a cup of
Living
Water

for a hurting soul

By David R. Veerman
& Neil S. Wilson

TYNDALE HOUSE PUBLISHERS, INC.
WHEATON, ILLINOIS

Visit Tyndale's exciting Web site at www.tyndale.com

A Cup of Living Water for a Hurting Soul copyright © 2001 by Tyndale House
Publishers, Inc. All rights reserved.

Material written and compiled by The Livingstone Corporation, Carol Stream, IL,
and the following individuals: Katherine Cloyd, indexer, and Joan Guest, editor.

Cover photograph copyright © 2001 by Kazutomo Kawai/Photonica. All rights
reserved.

Scripture quotations are taken from the *Holy Bible,* New Living Translation,
copyright © 1996. Used by permission of Tyndale House Publishers, Inc.,
Wheaton, Illinois 60189. All rights reserved.

New Living Translation and the New Living Translation logo are registered
trademarks of Tyndale House Publishers, Inc.

ISBN 0-8423-5563-6

Printed in the United States of America

05   04   03   02
5   4   3   2   1

Contents

Introduction

Cups of living water come in two forms: those given and those received. Jesus himself made that point when He said, "And if you give even a cup of cold water to one of the least of my followers, you will surely be rewarded" (Matthew 10:42). He also remarked, "If anyone gives you even a cup of water because you belong to the Messiah, I assure you, that person will be rewarded" (Mark 9:41). Following Jesus includes giving cups of water to those in need as well as accepting cups of water from others when we are in need. And ultimately, living water has only one source: Jesus Christ.

Living Water

So what is living water? When Jesus used that term in a conversation with a hurting woman (John 4:4-26), he wasn't inventing a new concept (Proverbs 18:4; Isaiah 58:11; Ezekiel 47:1-12). The Old Testament prophet Jeremiah recorded the expression twice. First, God described himself this way: "My people have done two evil things: They have forsaken me—the fountain of living water. And they have dug for themselves cracked cisterns that can hold no water at all!" (Jeremiah 2:13). Later, Jeremiah used the phrase in a prayer: "O LORD, the hope of Israel, all who turn away from you will be disgraced and shamed. They will be buried in a dry and dusty grave, for they have forsaken the LORD, the fountain of living water" (Jeremiah 17:13). In lands where water and life are daily concerns, the idea of living water draws immediate interest.

Centuries later, Jesus began his conversation with the woman at the well with a request for water. The Lord of the universe placed himself in debt to a sinful, outcast woman. He honored and shocked her by addressing her in the first place and by asking for her help. What a novel concept! Jesus disarmed her defenses against his help by seeking her help.

The woman's curiosity overcame her reserve and pain. She began to ask him questions: "Why are you asking me for a drink?" and "Where would you get this living water?" Eventually, she was able to receive living water from Jesus, the "man who told me everything I ever did!" (John 4:29). The living water flows from the living Word, and it does have an uncanny way of telling us everything we ever did. It also tells us everything that has been done for us! In spite of her hurts and even though what Jesus had to say to her included hard things, this woman found in Jesus someone she could trust with her hurting soul.

Not long after that episode in Samaria, Jesus announced to the crowds in Jerusalem that he was the source of living water for them. "If you are thirsty, come to me! If you believe in me, come and drink! For the Scriptures declare that rivers of living water will flow out from within" (John

5

7:37-38). John explains that Jesus was speaking of the Holy Spirit, who would be given to those who believe (John 7:39).

Are You a Hurting Soul?

Hurts are wounds to the soul that result from various experiences in life. Some are self-inflicted. Poor choices, even when corrected and forgiven, often leave behind tender scars on our inner person. Other injuries are inflicted on us through relationships with other people. Some are caused by disappointments and frustrations as we pursue life. And some seem to occur by painful mystery, bleeding sores that appear on our soul, unexpected and unexplained. Events in life that are supposed to be happy have the uncanny effect of revealing hurts. Who hasn't spent part of Christmas Day or a birthday affected by an undiagnosed soul-pain? Parents who cry at weddings often chalk up their tears to the joy of the occasion, but they are also nagged by a sense of loss as a child moves into a new phase of life.

All of the above can describe a hurting soul. At any one time in life, most of us are nursing at least one or two wounds within. Jesus was talking to hurting souls when he said, "Come to me, all of you who are weary and carry heavy burdens, and I will give you rest. Take my yoke upon you. Let me teach you, because I am humble and gentle, and you will find rest for your souls. For my yoke fits perfectly, and the burden I give you is light" (Matthew 11:28-30).

The care, nursing, and healing of a hurting soul

begins and continues with Jesus and his Word. If you desire to grow in spiritual health and preserve your joy, you must rely on continual input from God through his Word. The living water that flows out of you will be the living water that flows into you.

How to Use These Cups and Sips of Living Water

The cups of living water in these pages represent both forms of living water: some for you to receive and some for you to pass on after you receive them. Take time to reflect after each reading. Consider what God is offering you in each soul-satisfying drink of his living water. Then ask him to direct you to someone else who might find help from those same words. And don't forget the pattern Jesus sometimes used—helping others by asking for their help.

Drink deeply and continuously from our source of living water, the Holy Spirit, who lives in all those who believe in Jesus Christ.

a cup of . . .

Acceptance

LIVING WATER

The LORD your God is the God of gods and Lord of lords. He is the great God, mighty and awesome, who shows no partiality and takes no bribes.

DEUTERONOMY 10:17

Peter replied, "I see very clearly that God doesn't show partiality. In every nation he accepts those who fear him and do what is right." ACTS 10:34-35

There will be trouble and calamity for everyone who keeps on sinning—for the Jew first and also for the Gentile. But there will be glory and honor and peace from God for all who do good—for the Jew first and also for the Gentile. For God does not show favoritism. ROMANS 2:9-11

Thirst-quenching thought for the day

We're used to people playing favorites. Teachers have "pets," bosses have "fast-track employees," and just about everyone has a "best friend." And remember those days when kids would choose up sides for playground games? The "good" players were chosen first, and no one wanted to be chosen last.

Considering our experience, we might assume that God acts the same way—that he favors certain people because of their ability, personality, or another identifying characteristic. This assumption may lead us to wonder about God's feelings toward us and, perhaps, even to doubt our relationship with him.

But God revealed the truth to Peter: He doesn't play favorites for us or against us. Instead, he accepts people "from every nation." God acts out of grace and mercy toward us. The only qualification for acceptance and favor is that we honor, revere ("fear"), and obey him.

Sip to take away

Are you feeling rejected, put-down, or alone? Know that God accepts you and stands by you. And through Jesus, he gives you eternal life, regardless of your race, class, or sex. He has chosen you.

a cup of . . .

Adoption by God

LIVING WATER

You should not be like cowering, fearful slaves. You should behave instead like God's very own children, adopted into his family—calling him "Father, dear Father." For his Holy Spirit speaks to us deep in our hearts and tells us that we are God's children.

ROMANS 8:15-16

When the right time came, God sent his Son . . . to buy freedom for us who were slaves to the law, so that he could adopt us as his very own children. And because you Gentiles have become his children, God has sent the Spirit of his Son into your hearts, and now you can call God your dear Father. Now you are no longer a slave but God's own child. GALATIANS 4:4-7

See how very much our heavenly Father loves us, for he allows us to be called his children, and we really are! 1 JOHN 3:1

Thirst-quenching
thought for the day

Remember limping into the house after falling and scraping your knee? "Daddy!" you cried, hoping that somehow he would make everything right. Then Daddy would pick you up in his strong arms, wipe your tears, and hold you close. You felt secure, warm, and loved.

Many years have passed, and although you have grown, you still stumble and fall—in relationships, in business, in the home. And it still hurts terribly. At those times you long to have a loving parent hug you and kiss the pain away.

That's what it means to call God "dear Father." When you put your faith in Christ, you became a child of God, born (1 Peter 1:23) and adopted (Romans 8:15) into his family. Now you have all the rights and privileges of a child of the King. You can approach God anytime with your needs, hurts, and concerns. Whatever your struggle, he will help. Whatever your question, he will understand. Whatever your pain, he will comfort. He's your Father; he loves you.

Sip to take away

Do you still act like a stranger or, worse yet, a slave, cringing before a tyrannical master? Know the truth—you can call God "Daddy"!

a cup of . . .

Approachability

LIVING WATER

Because of Christ and our faith in him, we can now come fearlessly into God's presence, assured of his glad welcome.   EPHESIANS 3:12

Let us come boldly to the throne of our gracious God. There we will receive his mercy, and we will find grace to help us when we need it.   HEBREWS 4:16

Dear brothers and sisters, we can boldly enter heaven's Most Holy Place because of the blood of Jesus.   HEBREWS 10:19

Thirst-quenching thought for the day

Consider how you would feel if you were summoned to appear before the president of the United States. Certainly you would be apprehensive and intimidated by the power of the office and all the presidential trappings. Certainly you would consider it a rare privilege to meet the most powerful and influential person in the world.

With all that the office represents, however, the power and prestige of the president is nothing compared with that of almighty God, the Creator and Sustainer of the universe. Now consider how you would feel meeting him face-to-face.

But here's the incredible news: you can approach God with freedom and confidence. Because of Christ's work on the cross, you can enter God's presence through prayer. What an awesome privilege!

Freedom: You can talk with God about anything and everything. You can tell him about other people, ask for help, and even admit your doubts and failures.

Confidence: You can talk to God boldly, without fear of condemnation. God wants to hear from you.

Sip to take away

Whatever your need or situation, talk with God about it. He's approachable.

a cup of . . .

Awakening

LIVING WATER

Listen to my voice in the morning, LORD.
    Each morning I bring my requests to you and
        wait expectantly.   PSALM 5:3

As for me, I will sing about your power.
    I will shout with joy each morning because of
        your unfailing love.
For you have been my refuge,
    a place of safety in the day of distress.   PSALM 59:16

Great is his faithfulness; his mercies begin afresh
each day.   LAMENTATIONS 3:23

Thirst-quenching
thought for the day

David tells us that each morning he would spend time worshiping the Lord and presenting his needs. Then David would "wait," fully expecting God to fulfill his requests. David wasn't simply moving through a daily religious ritual. Confident that God was listening, David had very personal discussions with his loving Father, and he knew he could "wait in expectation." He even anticipated the new day as an opportunity to praise God!

Although God wants his people to talk with him continually through the day (see 1 Thessalonians 5:16-18), we need special times of deep conversation with him, confessing our sins, sharing our feelings, and presenting our requests. Spending time with God in the morning gives us the whole day to think about the conversation and to watch him answer our prayers.

Sip to take away

Whenever you talk with God, know that he is listening—he hears your voice. Share your thoughts, feelings, and needs with him, and expect him to answer you.

a cup of . . .
Being with Us

LIVING WATER

O Israel, the LORD who created you says: "Do not be afraid, for I have ransomed you. I have called you by name; you are mine. When you go through deep waters and great trouble, I will be with you. When you go through rivers of difficulty, you will not drown! When you walk through the fire of oppression, you will not be burned up; the flames will not consume you. For I am the LORD, your God, the Holy One of Israel, your Savior. . . . I am the LORD, and there is no other Savior. First I predicted your deliverance; I declared what I would do, and then I did it—I saved you. No foreign god has ever done this before. You are witnesses that I am the only God," says the LORD. "From eternity to eternity I am God. No one can oppose what I do. No one can reverse my actions."   ISAIAH 43:1-3, 11-13

Thirst-quenching thought for the day

Through the prophet Isaiah, God promised the people of Judah that he would be with them in every circumstance and through every trial. They were his. He had redeemed and called his people, and he would keep them safe and secure.

Through Christ, you too belong to God, so this promise belongs to you as well.

What deep waters of tragedy and sorrow do you face? You are not alone—God is with you.

What rivers of conflict and difficulty swirl around you, threatening to engulf and carry you away? Do not fear—God will take you through.

What fires lick at your heels? Keep walking—God will shield you from the flames.

Sip to take away

Keep going, knowing that you belong to God, the Holy One, your Savior.

a cup of . . .
Blessing

LIVING WATER

The LORD said to Moses, "Instruct Aaron and his sons to bless the people of Israel with this special blessing:

'May the LORD bless you
*   and protect you.*
May the LORD smile on you
*   and be gracious to you.*
May the LORD show you his favor
*   and give you his peace.' "*

This is how Aaron and his sons will designate the Israelites as my people, and I myself will bless them."

NUMBERS 6:22-27

You will be blessed wherever you go, both in coming and in going.   DEUTERONOMY 28:6

Thirst-quenching
thought for the day

This benediction often concludes church services.
Unfortunately, much like the expression "God bless
you" after a sneeze, this benediction has become
trivialized by familiarity. We really don't think
much about how we are "blessed," but God's blessings touch all of life. Consider these statements:

> "protect you"–connects God's blessing with
> protection.

> "May the LORD smile on you"–illustrates a close,
> loving relationship with God.

> "be gracious"–requests God's forgiveness and
> kindness, though it is undeserved.

> "give you peace"–anticipates inner strength,
> resolve, and confidence for living in
> tumultuous times.

Certainly these blessings contain much of what
we really want God to do in our lives. But the key
statement is, "This is how Aaron and his sons will
designate the Israelites as my people." People who
belong to God are blessed!

Sip to take away

Do you belong to God? Do you bear his
name? This passage is for you. Know that
you are blessed.

19

a cup of . . .

Childlikeness

LIVING WATER

The LORD protects those of childlike faith;
  I was facing death, and then he saved me.
Now I can rest again,
  for the LORD has been so good to me.
He has saved me from death,
  my eyes from tears,
  my feet from stumbling.
And so I walk in the LORD's presence
  as I live here on earth!   PSALM 116:6-9

I have stilled and quieted myself,
  just as a small child is quiet with its mother.
  Yes, like a small child is my soul within me.

                                        PSALM 131:1-2

Thirst-quenching thought for the day

One of the strong themes of the Psalms is God's loving care for us as his children. David and the other psalmists continually praised the Lord for his goodness, faithfulness, and deliverance.

Two concepts stand out in these passages. The first, "I can rest," or "I have stilled and quieted myself," describes the response of those who know God and truly trust him for salvation. The second, "for the Lord has been so good to me," describes the foundation for the first. As a person walks in God's presence, he or she can "rest" (relax) in his love and can live with childlike confidence. That person can become "stilled" and quiet before God, experiencing in the deepest sense what it means to know God as Father.

Sip to take away

Always remember that you are living in the presence of your loving, holy, and almighty God. He is with you, guarding and guiding. Then you will be able to relax in his love and live with peace.

a cup of . . .

Christ's Victory

LIVING WATER

He will swallow up death forever! The Sovereign LORD will wipe away all tears. He will remove forever all insults and mockery against his land and people. The LORD has spoken!   ISAIAH 25:8

Christ must reign until he humbles all his enemies beneath his feet. And the last enemy to be destroyed is death. . . . When this happens—when our perishable earthly bodies have been transformed into heavenly bodies that will never die—then at last the Scriptures will come true:

"Death is swallowed up in victory.
O death, where is your victory?
 O death, where is your sting?"

1 CORINTHIANS 15:25-26, 54-55

Thirst-quenching
thought for the day

Christ, our risen Savior, reigns as the King of kings and Lord of lords. Against him no enemy can stand—not Satan or sin or even death.

It's natural to fear death. Death looms as the certain but mysterious fate of every living creature. That insidious thief can appear without warning, at any time and in any place, robbing us of friendship, love, companionship, and joy. We fear for our own lives, but we also fear the deaths of those we love. If only death were like a trip that one could experience and then live to tell the story. But no one returns from the dead by his or her own power.

Except for one Person. Jesus died and then conquered death, rising to life again. And he brings new life and hope and peace to all who trust in him.

Sip to take away

In your sorrow, look to Jesus. He offers hope beyond the grave.

In your fear, turn to Jesus. He will quiet your storm and bring you safely to the shore.

In your pain, lean on Jesus. He defeated death and will carry you through.

a cup of . . .
Cleansing

LIVING WATER

Finally, I confessed all my sins to you
  and stopped trying to hide them.
I said to myself, "I will confess my rebellion
   to the LORD."
  And you forgave me! All my guilt is gone.

PSALM 32:5

Under the old system, the blood of goats and bulls and the ashes of a young cow could cleanse people's bodies from ritual defilement. Just think how much more the blood of Christ will purify our hearts from deeds that lead to death so that we can worship the living God. For by the power of the eternal Spirit, Christ offered himself to God as a perfect sacrifice for our sins.

HEBREWS 9:13-14

If we confess our sins to him, he is faithful and just to forgive us and to cleanse us from every wrong.

1 JOHN 1:9

Thirst-quenching thought for the day

Sin becomes a terrible burden to bear, stooping the shoulders, bending the knees, breaking the heart. Yet men and women continue, day after day, trying to carry that soul-crushing load, desperately needing help, relief, and forgiveness.

Why continue to struggle beneath the load of sin when the sin-bearer is near? Jesus, God's own Son, took our sins on himself as he hung on the Roman cross. He died so that we might live. He became sin so that we could be free from our sins. All we must do is turn to him in faith, confessing our failures, our disobedience, our shortcomings. With just a prayer, God lifts the load, forgives us, and makes us pure and free.

Sip to take away

Feeling weighed down with sin? Turn to Jesus. His forgiveness will lift the weight.

a cup of . . .

Closeness

LIVING WATER

Even when I walk
   through the dark valley of death,
I will not be afraid,
   for you are close beside me.
Your rod and your staff
   protect and comfort me.   PSALM 23:4

Even if my father and mother abandon me,
   the LORD will hold me close.   PSALM 27:10

The LORD is close to all who call on him,
   yes, to all who call on him sincerely.
He fulfills the desires of those who fear him;
   he hears their cries for help and rescues them.

                                        PSALM 145:18-19

Thirst-quenching thought for the day

In comic strips and cartoons, masked superheroes answer calls for help from those in distress. They rush quickly to the rescue just when all seems lost. We know, of course, that such characters exist only in fiction and in our imaginations. But at times, we want the cartoons to be true, especially when we are facing complex issues, giant problems, and difficult conflicts. We want someone to hear our frantic cries and run to our side.

These passages in Psalms declare that, in fact, someone is listening. Someone is close. Not an imaginary hero with superhuman powers, but a real Person with all power and authority (see Matthew 28:18). The Lord Almighty stands near, ready to save. And more than simply rescuing individuals from today's troubles, the Lord saves for all eternity.

Sip to take away

God knows your situation and your desires. He will fulfill your deepest needs. "The Lord is close"; he stands near and ready to help. God listens for you. He hears your cries, and he will save you.

a cup of . . .

Comfort

LIVING WATER

The needy will not be forgotten forever;
     the hopes of the poor will not always be crushed.

PSALM 9:18

I wait quietly before God,
     for my hope is in him.   PSALM 62:5

O Lord, you alone are my hope.
     I've trusted you, O LORD, from childhood.
Yes, you have been with me from birth;
     from my mother's womb you have cared for me.
No wonder I am always praising you!

PSALM 71:5-6

Thirst-quenching thought for the day

Remember when, as a little child, you became separated from your mother in the department store? All you saw were tall strangers and merchandise stacked to the ceiling as you panicked and rushed from aisle to aisle. Nothing is as frightening as the feeling of being lost and abandoned.

Although you are now a "grown-up," you can still feel forgotten and lost at times—especially when you are afflicted by illness or difficulty and can't find a single soul who can help you. So you are left feeling vulnerable and afraid.

But listen to words of the psalmist, who reminds us of a great promise from our loving Lord. Although you may be virtually invisible in this world, God sees you—he has not forgotten. Although the future looks dismal today, God continues to give you his promise of hope for tomorrow.

Sip to take away
You are not lost or forgotten. Look up and find God, and look ahead—to eternity—and find hope.

a cup of . . .

Community

LIVING WATER

They joined with the other believers and devoted
themselves to the apostles' teaching and fellowship,
sharing in the Lord's Supper and in prayer.   ACTS 2:42

Is there any encouragement from belonging to Christ?
Any comfort from his love? Any fellowship together in
the Spirit? Are your hearts tender and sympathetic?
Then make me truly happy by agreeing wholeheart-
edly with each other, loving one another, and working
together with one heart and purpose.   PHILIPPIANS 2:1-2

Let us not neglect our meeting together, as some
people do, but encourage and warn each other, espe-
cially now that the day of his coming back again is
drawing near.   HEBREWS 10:25

Thirst-quenching
thought for the day

When dealing with a difficult problem or tragedy, people often pull back from others and isolate themselves. Yet it is during these times of suffering that we need others the most, especially friends who will listen, comfort, affirm, counsel, and point us to Christ.

That is exactly what the church should be—a place where believers can encourage and strengthen each other and find acceptance and love and God's grace.

According to the passage from Hebrews, some believers had gotten away from their churchgoing habit. But the writer comments that these people needed the body of Christ more than ever, considering their proximity to the day of Christ's return.

Today we stand even closer to that day, and more than ever we need others who know us and who know the Lord. We need to meet together regularly for worship, instruction, fellowship, challenge, and strengthening.

Sip to take away
What keeps you from your Christian brothers and sisters?
Don't stay away.

a cup of . . .

Companionship

LIVING WATER

*There are "friends" who destroy each other, but a real
friend sticks closer than a brother.* PROVERBS 18:24

*Two people can accomplish more than twice as
much as one; they get a better return for their labor.
If one person falls, the other can reach out and help.
But people who are alone when they fall are in real
trouble. . . . A person standing alone can be attacked
and defeated, but two can stand back-to-back and
conquer. Three are even better, for a triple-braided
cord is not easily broken.* ECCLESIASTES 4:9-10, 12

Thirst-quenching
thought for the day

In these few lines, Solomon highlights the value of friendships. Friends work together, help each other, defend one another, and encourage each other. In contrast, the person without any friends must face the world alone. We need friends to encourage and support us, to give feedback and hold us accountable, to console and counsel us, and to direct us to God.

At times we may feel as though we would rather go it alone; after all, friendships require maintenance, and that means work. But God has created us as relational beings (Genesis 2:18), and he wants us to share his love with others, not to keep it to ourselves (1 Corinthians 13). He promises to be our friend, one who "sticks closer than a brother."

Sip to take away
Friends are gifts from God. Receive his gifts with gratitude, and be a gift to someone who needs a friend.

a cup of . . .
Compassion

LIVING WATER

The LORD still waits for you to come to him so he can show you his love and compassion. For the LORD is a faithful God. Blessed are those who wait for him to help them. ISAIAH 30:18

Sing for joy, O heavens! Rejoice, O earth! Burst into song, O mountains! For the LORD has comforted his people and will have compassion on them in their sorrow. ISAIAH 49:13

"For a brief moment I abandoned you, but with great compassion I will take you back. In a moment of anger I turned my face away for a little while. But with everlasting love I will have compassion on you," says the LORD, your Redeemer. ISAIAH 54:7-8

Thirst-quenching thought for the day

Isaiah brought bad news and good news to God's people. The bad news was that they would be conquered, defeated, and taken captive by a foreign power. But the good news was that, eventually, the nation would be restored. The best news was that whether they were captive or free, God would be with them, giving them comfort and hope.

Do you feel hemmed in, trapped, a captive to your unrelenting schedule and assaulted by a host of enemies who threaten to steal your joy? Or do you feel desperate as you struggle with physical pain, financial demands, or interpersonal conflicts? Listen to God's Word. Isaiah tells us that the Lord comforts his people and "will have compassion on them in their sorrow." He hasn't forgotten you; in fact, he sees you right now and knows what you are going through.

Sip to take away
Make your next move toward him, and then shout, rejoice, and burst into song!

a cup of . . .
Confidence

LIVING WATER

As for me, I know that my Redeemer lives, and that he will stand upon the earth at last. And after my body has decayed, yet in my body I will see God! I will see him for myself. Yes, I will see him with my own eyes. I am overwhelmed at the thought!

JOB 19:25-27

I know the one in whom I trust, and I am sure that he is able to guard what I have entrusted to him until the day of his return.

2 TIMOTHY 1:12

Yes, dear friends, we are already God's children, and we can't even imagine what we will be like when Christ returns. But we do know that when he comes we will be like him, for we will see him as he really is.

1 JOHN 3:2

Thirst-quenching
thought for the day

Job had lost all his children, his livestock, and his possessions. His wife had reacted by telling him to "curse God and die" (Job 2:9). Next, Job was afflicted with boils. Then his friends showed up and began spewing useless counsel and accusations of unnamed sins. Job's natural reaction would have been to become embittered and take his wife's advice.

But Job's faith was rooted in God and not in his situation and surroundings. He knew that his Redeemer was alive and in control. Despite Job's terrible physical and emotional pain, he could look beyond his circumstances to the Lord, and beyond his present condition to the future.

Few, if any, have suffered as much as Job or expressed such deep faith. Paul and John echo Job's simple assurance, which is rooted in Christ.

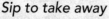 *Sip to take away*
What pain do you endure? Learn with Job that God can meet you in your need. As Corrie ten Boom stated, "No matter how deep the pit, God is deeper still." Now that is true confidence in God.

a cup of...

Consolation

Living Water

God blesses those who mourn,
   for they will be comforted.   MATTHEW 5:4

To all who mourn in Israel, he will give beauty for
ashes, joy instead of mourning, praise instead of
despair. For the LORD has planted them like strong
and graceful oaks for his own glory.   ISAIAH 61:3

All praise to the God and Father of our Lord Jesus
Christ. He is the source of every mercy and the God
who comforts us. He comforts us in all our troubles
so that we can comfort others. When others are trou-
bled, we will be able to give them the same comfort
God has given us. You can be sure that the more we
suffer for Christ, the more God will shower us with
his comfort through Christ.   2 CORINTHIANS 1:3-5

Thirst-quenching
thought for the day

"Why?" we silently shout to God as we stand by the grave of a loved one. Overwhelmed by grief, we may question God's goodness and wonder how he could allow such suffering and pain. Death seems such a defeat.

Each day brings a multitude of reasons for discouragement and despair—lost dreams, broken promises, hurt feelings, persecution, misunderstanding, disease, war, natural disaster. Even Jesus endured many of these things while he was here on earth. He experienced the death of a dear friend (Lazarus), rejection by family and friends, physical and verbal abuse from religious leaders, disappointment with inconsistent disciples, betrayal by a close associate, and the ultimate rejection of society.

Yet Jesus said that God blesses those who mourn. Jesus knew that this life is not all there is, and that one day those who trust in him will find deep comfort, profound peace, and unending joy in God's presence.

 ### Sip to take away
Whatever the cause, let your mourning push you toward the Savior. You will be blessed.

a cup of . . .

Covenant Promises

Living Water

*I will remember my covenant with you and with
everything that lives. Never again will there be a
flood that will destroy all life. When I see the rain-
bow in the clouds, I will remember the eternal covenant between God and every living creature on
earth.* Genesis 9:15-16

*I will remember my covenant with Jacob, with Isaac,
and with Abraham, and I will remember the land. . . .
I will remember my ancient covenant with their
ancestors, whom I brought out of Egypt while all the
nations watched. I, the Lord, am their God.*
Leviticus 26:42, 45

*Remember, O my God, all that I have done for these
people, and bless me for it.* Nehemiah 5:19

Thirst-quenching
thought for the day

Three times in the Leviticus verses God refers to covenant, and three times he says that he "will remember."

People forget. We forget names, places, and even promises. We even use forgetting as an excuse, as in "I just forgot."

But God remembers. He remembers people ("Isaac," "Abraham," and even "their ancestors"), places ("the land"), and especially his covenant promises. And he remembers you. Notice God's promise in Genesis. After all, are you not among "every living creature on earth"? This is the reason why Nehemiah repeatedly asked God to remember him. Nehemiah knew that God keeps his promises.

Sip to take away
Do you ever feel forgotten? You may wonder whether anybody knows or cares. God does. He remembers your name and his promise to be with you and to guide you. Now it's up to you to remember your Lord and his love for you, and then to find hope in him.

a cup of . . .

Deep Roots

Living Water

Taste and see that the LORD is good.
Oh, the joys of those who trust in him!   PSALM 34:8

Oh, the joys of those who trust the LORD,
who have no confidence in the proud,
or in those who worship idols.   PSALM 40:4

But blessed are those who trust in the LORD and
have made the LORD their hope and confidence. They
are like trees planted along a riverbank, with roots
that reach deep into the water. Such trees are not
bothered by the heat or worried by long months of
drought. Their leaves stay green, and they go right
on producing delicious fruit.   JEREMIAH 17:7-8

Thirst-quenching thought for the day

Where do you place your trust? Where are your deepest roots? In family and friends? In money and possessions? In business? In government? Even your dearest loved ones and strongest institutions cannot supply your deepest needs. Without deep roots, you will wilt and wither like a parched plant in the heat of this sinful world.

Not so with God. Jeremiah pictures people who trust in God as strong trees bearing fruit year after year because they have been planted by a wise gardener. Their deep roots draw water from the life-giving stream that flows nearby.

In the same way, God knows what you need to nourish your soul—streams of living water—and he will plant you there if you let him. His supply will never run dry. Don't fear either heat or drought; trust in the Lord. You will be blessed. That's his promise!

Sip to take away

Ask the Lord to show you one specific action you could take today that would involve a deeper trust in him. Follow through on his direction.

a cup of . . .

Delight

LIVING WATER

Through each day the LORD pours his unfailing love
    upon me,
    and through each night I sing his songs,
    praying to God who gives me life. . . .
Why am I discouraged?
    Why so sad?
I will put my hope in God!
    I will praise him again—
    my Savior and my God!   PSALM 42:8, 11

The LORD delights in his people;
    he crowns the humble with salvation.
Let the faithful rejoice in this honor.
    Let them sing for joy as they lie on their beds.

                                    PSALM 149:4-5

Thirst-quenching
thought for the day

An unsettling report from the doctor, a lingering illness, a financial reversal, or a broken relationship—numerous setbacks and troubles can undermine our security and steal our dreams. All of this can cause us to be downcast and upset—even to the point of despair. Evidently something like this also happened to the writer of Psalm 42.

But, as the psalmist realized, focusing on our great God can renew our strength and courage. The wonderful truth is that the loving Father directs our ways and guides our steps during the day. And even at night, as we sleep, God still stands with us, watching over us and delighting in us. Thus, we see in these psalms that, as the attention of the writers turns to God, discouragement transforms to hope, and sorrow turns to praise.

Sip to take away

What troubling questions, doubts, and struggles threaten you? Take your eyes off your circumstances and turn to your Lord—look up instead of down. Then you will gain new hope, knowing that you are secure in God's loving arms and that his delight is in you.

a cup of . . .

Direction

LIVING WATER

The law of the LORD is perfect,
reviving the soul.
The decrees of the LORD are trustworthy,
making wise the simple.
The commandments of the LORD are right,
bringing joy to the heart.
The commands of the LORD are clear,
giving insight to life.
Reverence for the LORD is pure,
lasting forever.
The laws of the LORD are true;
each one is fair.　　　　　　　PSALM 19:7-9

How can a young person stay pure?
By obeying your word and following its rules.
　　　　　　　　　　　　　　PSALM 119:9

Thirst-quenching thought for the day

A hurting soul that is truly on the mend doesn't seek an answer to the question, "How can I keep from getting hurt again?" as much as it seeks to discover, "How can I respond to life's trials the way God wants me to respond?" And the way to know what God wants is to read his book.

Check out God's laws, decrees, and commands. They are "perfect," "trustworthy," "right," "pure," and "true." In them you will discover God's clear direction for living. And following them will bring revival, wisdom, joy, and light! They will prepare you to survive and thrive in spite of the hurts and trials of life.

Sip to take away

Don't lose your way in the fog of worldly values and human understanding. Study God's message, learn his truths, and follow his instruction. Then you will stay on the right road and move in the right direction.

a cup of . . .

Election

LIVING WATER

*How we praise God, the Father of our Lord Jesus
Christ, who has blessed us with every spiritual
blessing in the heavenly realms because we belong
to Christ. Long ago, even before he made the world,
God loved us and chose us in Christ to be holy and
without fault in his eyes.*   EPHESIANS 1:3-4

*We are thankful that God chose you to be among the
first to experience salvation, a salvation that came
through the Spirit who makes you holy and by your
belief in the truth.*   2 THESSALONIANS 2:13

*God the Father chose you long ago, and the Spirit
has made you holy. As a result, you have obeyed
Jesus Christ and are cleansed by his blood. May you
have more and more of God's special favor and
wonderful peace.*   1 PETER 1:2

Thirst-quenching thought for the day

The word chosen connotes being specially selected. Choice foods are of highest quality; the top draft choice is seen as the best athlete in his sport. Everyone wants to be chosen for the team or for an important position. Being chosen boosts one's self esteem. Conversely, not to be chosen can be interpreted as being ignored, passed over, or rejected outright. So consider what it would mean to be chosen, or elected, by God—selected, hand-picked, pointed out to be in his family, on his team.

That is precisely Paul and Peter's point in these passages. All those who follow Christ are God's specially chosen people. In fact, they were chosen "before he made the world." No wonder Paul says that we have been blessed "with every spiritual blessing in the heavenly realms because we belong to Christ."

Sip to take away

When you feel neglected and rejected, when your self-esteem droops and you begin to feel unwanted and worthless, remember God's powerful statement through Paul—you are one of his chosen people. Praise God!

a cup of . . .

Empathy

LIVING WATER

Your attitude should be the same that Christ Jesus had. Though he was God, he did not demand and cling to his rights as God. He made himself nothing; he took the humble position of a slave and appeared in human form. And in human form he obediently humbled himself even further by dying a criminal's death on a cross. PHILIPPIANS 2:5-8

It was necessary for Jesus to be in every respect like us, his brothers and sisters, so that he could be our merciful and faithful High Priest before God. He then could offer a sacrifice that would take away the sins of the people. Since he himself has gone through suffering and temptation, he is able to help us when we are being tempted. HEBREWS 2:17-18

Thirst-quenching thought for the day

It's easy to accuse God of not understanding our plight, especially when we hurt deeply and struggle for answers. God can seem so far away, so removed from the reality of our daily problems and questions. And during our pain we may question his love and justice.

In this powerful passage to the Philippians, however, Paul reminds us that God is not aloof, above and beyond our struggles. The writer of Hebrews echoes that truth. In fact, two thousand years ago Jesus, the fully divine Son of God, humbled himself and became a living, breathing baby, totally dependent upon his mother. The baby grew and matured to become a little boy, then a teenager, and then a man. Eventually, the Son's identification with us humans led to his suffering and death, for he was mocked, tortured, and finally crucified. The least likely candidate, the innocent and pure Son of God, was executed like a notorious criminal.

Sip to take away
Whatever your hurt, remember Jesus. He understands and sympathizes, because he knows what you are going through—he lived it.

a cup of . . .
Eternal Life

LIVING WATER

God so loved the world that he gave his only Son, so that everyone who believes in him will not perish but have eternal life. JOHN 3:16

Now you are free from the power of sin and have become slaves of God. Now you do those things that lead to holiness and result in eternal life. For the wages of sin is death, but the free gift of God is eternal life through Christ Jesus our Lord. ROMANS 6:22-23

At the right time Christ will be revealed from heaven by the blessed and only almighty God, the King of kings and Lord of lords. He alone can never die, and he lives in light so brilliant that no human can approach him. No one has ever seen him, nor ever will. To him be honor and power forever. Amen.
1 TIMOTHY 6:15-16

Thirst-quenching
thought for the day

The one sure rule of life is that everything dies—grass, flowers, trees, insects, wild animals, pets, strangers, neighbors, and loved ones. No one escapes death. Accepting this chilling fact is difficult for some, especially the young, to whom a decade seems like forever. Eventually, however, each person must deal with his or her own mortality. This unpleasant thought becomes a painful reality with the passing of years. We long to live forever. However, Paul reminds us that Christ "alone can never die."

Paul's statement provides hope. The eternal King of kings and Lord of lords has the power to grant all that he has promised for those who trust in him: peace, power, purpose, protection, eternal life.

While we cannot fully understand our God, we can trust him. And he has promised that although we will surely die, we will also surely live again (John 11:25-26) and enjoy all that he has prepared for us (John 14:1-4).

Sip to take away
Whatever your struggle, take hope in this truth: God alone is immortal, and he will grant you eternal life with him.

a cup of . . .

Eternal Refreshment

LIVING WATER

The LORD will guide you continually, watering your life when you are dry and keeping you healthy, too. You will be like a well-watered garden, like an ever-flowing spring.   ISAIAH 58:11

Jesus replied, "People soon become thirsty again after drinking this water. But the water I give them takes away thirst altogether. It becomes a perpetual spring within them, giving them eternal life."

JOHN 4:13-14

On the last day, the climax of the festival, Jesus stood and shouted to the crowds, "If you are thirsty, come to me! If you believe in me, come and drink! For the Scriptures declare that rivers of living water will flow out from within."   JOHN 7:37-38

Thirst-quenching
thought for the day

When Jesus spoke with the Samaritan woman at the well (John 4:1-42), he offered her eternal life. Relating his offer to physical thirst, he described the "living water" he would provide as a continual spring, quenching thirst forever. Jesus could make this promise because he was God in the flesh—the Author of life and the Giver of eternal life. And when Jesus makes a promise, we can be sure that he will fulfill it. All those who drink will live forever.

Are you frustrated with this world with its pain and struggles? Remember, this life is not all there is.

Are you thirsty for meaning, purpose, and significance? Remember, water from Jesus will quench your longings and your deepest needs. Hear him calling out to you as he did in the crowd so long ago, "If you are thirsty, come to me."

Sip to take away

Have you visited numerous "wells" in your search for refreshment? Remember, Jesus alone is the source of the eternal spring!

a cup of...
Everlasting Arms

LIVING WATER

The eternal God is your refuge,
*   and his everlasting arms are under you.*
He thrusts out the enemy before you;
*   it is he who cries, "Destroy them!"*

DEUTERONOMY 33:27

The LORD is a shelter for the oppressed,
*   a refuge in times of trouble.*
Those who know your name trust in you,
*   for you, O LORD, have never abandoned anyone*
*   who searches for you.*   PSALM 9:9-10

Lord, through all the generations
*   you have been our home!*   PSALM 90:1

Thirst-quenching thought for the day

Just before Israel moved into the Promised Land and just before his death, Moses blessed the nation of Israel (see Deuteronomy 33:1). The blessing for the tribe of Asher promises that God will keep them safe, held securely in his "everlasting arms."

Picture a strong, young shepherd carrying a frightened lamb to the safety of the fold, crossing swirling river waters during a storm. The shepherd's steps are sure, and his hold on the lamb is strong.

Or picture a father lifting his child and pulling her close in a loving embrace, wiping her tears and assuring her that all is well.

That's God—loving, strong, and always there. His arms hold us securely and eternally. They never let go. The word that names our need is refuge, a description that fits God better than anyone or anything else. He is our ultimate refuge.

Sip to take away

What enemies threaten you today? What dangers surround you? Live by faith, confidently resting in your Father's "everlasting arms."

a cup of...

Fairness

LIVING WATER

Speak up for those who cannot speak for them-selves; ensure justice for those who are perishing. Yes, speak up for the poor and helpless, and see that they get justice. PROVERBS 31:8-9

Learn to do good. Seek justice. Help the oppressed. Defend the orphan. Fight for the rights of widows.
ISAIAH 1:17

This is what the LORD says: Be fair-minded and just. Do what is right! Help those who have been robbed; rescue them from their oppressors. Quit your evil deeds! Do not mistreat foreigners, orphans, and widows. Stop murdering the innocent! JEREMIAH 22:3

Thirst-quenching thought for the day

The theme of justice runs through the Bible—God is concerned that people be treated with fairness in our world. It also is clear that he expects his people to encourage, defend, and plead for those who are not being treated fairly—especially those who cannot defend themselves. When you come in contact with the oppressed or with orphans or widows, do you think, What can we do to seek justice for them?

At the same time, we can find rest in knowing that God wants justice for us, too. We can be confident that he will watch over us when we are oppressed and when we lose father, mother, or spouse. He will be fighting for us and will be with us through it all, encouraging us, defending us, and acting in our behalf.

Sip to take away

So when you feel abused, treated unfairly, or alone, when you feel as though no one cares, remember that you serve a God who seeks justice for the oppressed. And remember to look out for those who need someone to defend them as well.

a cup of . . .

Faithful Love

LIVING WATER

Give thanks to the LORD, for he is good!
  His faithful love endures forever.   PSALM 107:1

Give thanks to the LORD, for he is good!
  His faithful love endures forever.
Give thanks to the God of gods.
  His faithful love endures forever.
Give thanks to the Lord of lords.
  His faithful love endures forever. . . .
Give thanks to the God of heaven.
  His faithful love endures forever.   PSALM 136:1-3, 26

Thirst-quenching
thought for the day

Do you remember young love? When it was over, you thought your heart would break. Do you remember being betrayed by one you thought was a friend? Angry and bitter, you wondered how to respond. Have you ever been the boss's favorite employee and then fallen out of favor? Disillusioned, you probably entertained thoughts of quitting.

Our God is not like other gods or lords. He is good, perfectly good, and his love differs infinitely from human affection—his love lasts.

Twenty-six times in Psalm 136 the writer repeats the amazing truth, "His faithful love endures forever." Whether it was meant as a worship response or a poetic refrain, this phrase serves as a powerful reminder that should be repeated daily.

Sip to take away

When grieving a loss, remember: God's faithful love endures forever.

When struggling for answers, remember: Your Lord's faithful love endures forever.

When feeling abandoned and alone, remember: The Father's faithful love endures forever.

a cup of . . .
Family

LIVING WATER

You are all children of God through faith in Christ Jesus. And all who have been united with Christ in baptism have been made like him. There is no longer Jew or Gentile, slave or free, male or female. For you are all Christians—you are one in Christ Jesus.

GALATIANS 3:26-28

Christ himself has made peace between us Jews and you Gentiles by making us all one people. He has broken down the wall of hostility that used to separate us. By his death he ended the whole system of Jewish law that excluded the Gentiles. His purpose was to make peace between Jews and Gentiles by creating in himself one new person from the two groups. Together as one body, Christ reconciled both groups to God by means of his death, and our hostility toward each other was put to death.

EPHESIANS 2:14-16

Thirst-quenching
thought for the day

Differences divide families, neighborhoods, communities, and nations. Differences in race, nationality, culture, social strata, language, gender, and skin color push people from each other. The news media continually report stories of civil unrest, hate crimes, bigotry, terrorism, and ethnic cleansing. It seems the more we become a global village, the more we splinter and divide.

These passages, however, describe a quite different situation. "In Christ" there is togetherness, oneness, unity. And instead of conflict, there is peace.

People of both genders and all races, nations, and backgrounds are invited into God's family. Acceptance into his family is based only on Christ and what he has done. All who follow him are welcome.

Sip to take away

If you have ever felt the sting of prejudice and the loneliness of rejection, you know that this passage shouts good news. You are accepted and loved now, by God and your brothers and sisters, and one day we will all live together in heaven.

a cup of . . .

Fear of God

LIVING WATER

I know that whatever God does is final. Nothing can be added to it or taken from it. God's purpose in this is that people should fear him. ECCLESIASTES 3:14

Even though a person sins a hundred times and still lives a long time, I know that those who fear God will be better off. The wicked will never live long, good lives, for they do not fear God. Their days will never grow long like the evening shadows.

ECCLESIASTES 8:12-13

Here is my final conclusion: Fear God and obey his commands, for this is the duty of every person. God will judge us for everything we do, including every secret thing, whether good or bad. ECCLESIASTES 12:13-14

Thirst-quenching thought for the day

"This is the duty of every person," says the writer of Ecclesiastes. That's quite a statement. After chronicling his search for meaning and purpose in life, Solomon concluded that "the duty of every person" is to "fear God and obey his commands."

Solomon wrote this under the inspiration of the Holy Spirit. From a human perspective, people should seek pleasure, wealth, popularity, and power—success, according to the world. Solomon had achieved all of that and more, yet he summarized it all as empty, vain, "meaningless." Solomon had learned that spending a lifetime pursuing those goals just leads to moral and spiritual bankruptcy.

But looking at life from beyond a finite human experience, Solomon could see that, in reality, only God matters.

Sip to take away

Are you tired of endlessly pursuing goals that always seem to leave you unsatisfied once you've reached them? Like Solomon, focus your heart on God and his purposes and learn to fear him. He is what truly matters.

a cup of...

Fearlessness

LIVING WATER

The LORD is my light and my salvation—
   so why should I be afraid?
The LORD protects me from danger—
   so why should I tremble?   PSALM 27:1

*What can we say about such wonderful things as
these? If God is for us, who can ever be against us?*
                                           ROMANS 8:31

*"Don't be afraid!" Elisha told him. "For there are
more on our side than on theirs!" Then Elisha
prayed, "O LORD, open his eyes and let him see!" The
LORD opened his servant's eyes, and when he looked
up, he saw that the hillside around Elisha was filled
with horses and chariots of fire.*   2 KINGS 6:16-17

Thirst-quenching thought for the day

The Arameans had surrounded Dothan in an attempt to capture Elisha. When Elisha's servant discovered the enemy encamped around them, he exclaimed with fear, "Oh, my lord, what shall we do?" (2 Kings 6:15). That's when Elisha told him, "There are more on our side than on theirs!"

Then, with eyes opened by God, the servant looked again and saw the hills full of horses and chariots of fire—God's angelic army—encircling the enemy (6:17). Elisha and his servant had no need to fear.

Often enemies surround us. At times the opposing forces have faces and names. Often, however, the enemy is unseen but just as real—forces seeking to defeat the spirit, steal hope and joy, and ruin lives. That's when believers need eyes of faith to see God's infinite power and his mighty hosts encircling the enemy and guaranteeing ultimate security.

Sip to take away

Look at your enemies. Now look again—with eyes that see God at work on your behalf. See the hosts of heaven on your side. Then, with renewed confidence, serve your commander-in-chief fearlessly.

a cup of . . .

Fellowship

LIVING WATER

Jesus replied, "All those who love me will do what I say. My Father will love them, and we will come to them and live with them."　　　JOHN 14:23

You must remain faithful to what you have been taught from the beginning. If you do, you will continue to live in fellowship with the Son and with the Father. And in this fellowship we enjoy the eternal life he promised us.　　　1 JOHN 2:24-25

Look! Here I stand at the door and knock. If you hear me calling and open the door, I will come in, and we will share a meal as friends.　　　REVELATION 3:20

Thirst-quenching thought for the day

In this powerful picture from Revelation, Jesus stands at the door of the church and knocks. He wants to enter, to fellowship with the believers there. But Jesus doesn't force his way in, pounding at the door, prying it open, or knocking it down. Instead, he stands and politely knocks.

The church at Laodicea, to whom these words are addressed, had become lukewarm; that is, they had become enamored with themselves and their wealth instead. Eventually, Jesus was no longer with them. He stood on the outside, knocking, hoping to get their attention so that he might enter and change their lives. The other passages emphasize how much we lose when we grow away from God's truth.

Where is Jesus for you? Outside or in? Is he a stranger, or do you spend time together? What concerns occupy your thoughts and desires? Do they threaten to push Jesus aside and move him to the fringe of your life?

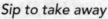

Sip to take away

Whatever your situation, know that the Lord is standing near. Hear his gentle knock. Push through the clutter and open the door. Welcome Christ in. It will make all the difference in the world.

a cup of . . .
Forgiveness

LIVING WATER

"Come now, let us argue this out," says the LORD.
"No matter how deep the stain of your sins, I can
remove it. I can make you as clean as freshly fallen
snow. Even if you are stained as red as crimson, I
can make you as white as wool."   ISAIAH 1:18

I—yes, I alone—am the one who blots out your sins
for my own sake and will never think of them again.
                                         ISAIAH 43:25

Let the people turn from their wicked deeds. Let
them banish from their minds the very thought of
doing wrong! Let them turn to the LORD that he may
have mercy on them. Yes, turn to our God, for he will
abundantly pardon.   ISAIAH 55:7

Thirst-quenching
thought for the day

Saying "I forgive you" comes easily, but truly forgiving and forgetting is much more difficult. Knowing our tendency to store past offenses and hold grudges, we assume that God does the same.

But these passages proclaim that God "will never think of them [your sins] again." Even the stain of our sins is so completely gone that, to God, we are as clean as freshly fallen snow.

Does God take sin seriously? Definitely! Sin is so serious that it deserves a penalty, eternal death (see Romans 6:23).

Does God forgive sinners? Certainly! God sent Jesus to take the punishment for sin, dying on the cross in our place. All who repent and trust in Christ can be forgiven (see John 3:17).

Can we trust God to forgive us? Of course! Since God did not spare even his own Son but gave him up for us all, won't God also give us everything else (Romans 8:32)?

Sip to take away

Release your load of guilt. Stand tall and allow God's forgiveness to wash you clean, and know that God's forgiveness makes you as pure as freshly fallen snow.

a cup of . . .
Friendship

LIVING WATER

*Friendship with the LORD is reserved for those who
    fear him.
    With them he shares the secrets of his covenant.*

*I no longer call you servants, because a master
doesn't confide in his servants. Now you are my
friends, since I have told you everything the Father
told me.*

JOHN 15:15

*Since we were restored to friendship with God by
the death of his Son while we were still his enemies,
we will certainly be delivered from eternal punishment by his life. So now we can rejoice in our
wonderful new relationship with God—all because
of what our Lord Jesus Christ has done for us in
making us friends of God.*

ROMANS 5:10-11

Thirst-quenching thought for the day

In his last teaching to his disciples before he was betrayed, Jesus explained that they should see themselves not as his servants, but as his friends. It is an important distinction. Good servants work hard for the master and are loyal and faithful. But they aren't privileged to know the master's plans, reasons, and motives. They simply must obey.

Friends, however, share experiences and information. They know each other well, and they move together in the same direction. Jesus had revealed to these men all that he had learned from his Father. They truly were his friends.

Twenty centuries later, we who name Christ as Savior also stand as his friends. He has given us the Bible, his written Word, to study and apply, and he has given us the Holy Spirit to teach us (John 14:26). We can know our Lord's business because we are his friends.

Sip to take away

When you feel all alone and don't know which way to turn, turn to God. He will answer, because Jesus has called you friend. He is always there when you need him, and he always will be.

a cup of . . .

Fulfillment

LIVING WATER

Since we have been made right in God's sight by faith, we have peace with God because of what Jesus Christ our Lord has done for us. Because of our faith, Christ has brought us into this place of highest privilege where we now stand, and we confidently and joyfully look forward to sharing God's glory. We can rejoice, too, when we run into problems and trials, for we know that they are good for us—they help us learn to endure. And endurance develops strength of character in us, and character strengthens our confident expectation of salvation. And this expectation will not disappoint us. For we know how dearly God loves us, because he has given us the Holy Spirit to fill our hearts with his love. ROMANS 5:1-5

Whenever trouble comes your way, let it be an opportunity for joy. For when your faith is tested, your endurance has a chance to grow. So let it grow, for when your endurance is fully developed, you will be strong in character and ready for anything. JAMES 1:2-4

Thirst-quenching thought for the day

These profound passages teach that those who know Christ have:

- Justification—they are "made right" because of what Christ has done on the cross;
- Peace—they are no longer at war with God;
- Hope—they are "confidently and joyfully" looking forward to a glorious future;
- Love—they are filled with God's presence;
- Perseverance—they have been tested and are able to stand strong and endure;
- Character—they are honest, dependable, and filled with integrity; and
- Joy—they can rejoice in God and his marvelous plan.

God sent these words, through Paul and James, to people familiar with struggles, hardship, and pain. And God encouraged these beleaguered Christians with these truths to give them hope and joy. These words of encouragement remain true today.

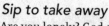

Sip to take away

Are you lonely? God gives his love. Do you struggle with conflicts and worries? God gives his peace. Have you reached the end of your resources? God gives his hope. Are you suffering? God gives his Spirit, working in you to develop perseverance and character.

a cup of . . .

God's Attentiveness

LIVING WATER

Come and listen, all you who fear God,
and I will tell you what he did for me.
For I cried out to him for help,
praising him as I spoke.
If I had not confessed the sin in my heart,
my Lord would not have listened.
But God did listen!
He paid attention to my prayer.
Praise God, who did not ignore my prayer
and did not withdraw his unfailing love from me.

PSALM 66:16-20

I love the LORD because he hears
and answers my prayers.
Because he bends down and listens,
I will pray as long as I have breath!   PSALM 116:1-2

Thirst-quenching thought for the day

New mothers seem to gain heightened hearing ability when their children are born. They can hear the baby's whimper from three rooms away through closed doors. Everyone else is oblivious to the cry, so they continue their conversation. But the mother hears it—her ears are tuned; her hearing is sensitive.

That's how the writer of these psalms pictures God. Bending down, listening to his people, God hears their cries, and he responds with mercy and grace.

It's easy to feel lost, alone, and anonymous in this noisy world where millions scream for attention. And when pain strikes and tough times come, our lonely feelings grow. We voice our silent pleas for help, but does anyone hear? Does anyone care?

God does. In fact, he has "paid attention" to us. He hears the cry; he feels the pain; he sends his love.

Sip to take away

In response to this great truth, the psalm writer professed to "love the Lord" and promised, "I will pray as long as I have breath." What do you say? How will you respond?

a cup of . . .

God's Changelessness

LIVING WATER

Your throne, O God, endures forever and ever.
  Your royal power is expressed in righteousness.

<small>HEBREWS 1:8</small>

*Jesus Christ is the same yesterday, today, and
forever.*

<small>HEBREWS 13:8</small>

*"I am the Alpha and the Omega—the beginning and
the end," says the Lord God. "I am the one who is,
who always was, and who is still to come, the
Almighty One."*

<small>REVELATION 1:8</small>

Thirst-quenching thought for the day

Change defines our world. Each day governments fall, children grow and mature, friends move away, storms uproot trees, new buildings replace old ones, colors fade, summer turns into fall, and technological advances render modern appliances obsolete. All these changes can begin to undermine our sense of security. We wonder, What will last? What is solid? Who will be there for me? We wonder who we can trust when once-close friends and associates renege on commitments and break promises.

Then we read these verses, which proclaim an amazing truth: Jesus Christ, the divine Son of God, who died for us and rose from the dead, does not change. In truth, he is the same as he has always been—loving, forgiving, merciful, and just. And Jesus is reliable—he keeps his promises. We can be sure that what he says, he will do. We can know that he will be with us and for us forever, just as he is today.

Sip to take away
Feeling unsure or insecure as you face the continuous challenge of change? Plant your feet and your faith on a solid foundation—your faithful Lord.

a cup of . . .

God's Fatherhood

LIVING WATER

Father to the fatherless, defender of widows—
   this is God, whose dwelling is holy.   PSALM 68:5

The LORD is like a father to his children,
   tender and compassionate to those who fear him.
                                          PSALM 103:13

"They will be my people," says the LORD Almighty.
"On the day when I act, they will be my own special
treasure. I will spare them as a father spares an
obedient and dutiful child."   MALACHI 3:17

Thirst-quenching
thought for the day

Throughout Scripture, God uses the word *father* to describe how he relates to his people. Through this intimate relationship, we learn both about God and about fathering. Thus, we can know how a good father should act by looking at how God relates to us, his children. Conversely, good human fathers provide a glimpse of God as they reflect his nature in their actions, as these passages attest.

Good fathers have compassion on their children. They don't overpower with authority, lead by intimidation, respond with bitterness and spite, or take pleasure in meting out punishment. Instead, they empathize with their children, hurting when they hurt; they lead tenderly and firmly, with love and by example; they temper judgment with mercy and are ready always to forgive and start afresh. God mirrors that example perfectly.

Sip to take away

Have you trusted Christ as Savior? Do you call God "Father"? Do you fear (respect) him? Then know that he deals with you with compassion. Admit you r frailties and confess your sins. Run to his embrace; give him your hand; let him teach you his ways and lead you on the path of righteousness.

a cup of . . .

God's Fullness

LIVING WATER

*My people have done two evil things: They have
forsaken me—the fountain of living water. And they
have dug for themselves cracked cisterns that can
hold no water at all!* JEREMIAH 2:13

*O LORD, the hope of Israel, all who turn away from
you will be disgraced and shamed. They will be
buried in a dry and dusty grave, for they have
forsaken the LORD, the fountain of living water.*
JEREMIAH 17:13

Thirst-quenching thought for the day

Those who live in the desert understand the need for water. They know that there is no better source for life-giving water than a spring or river. It would be strange indeed for a person living in the desert to ignore such an invaluable resource if it was freely available, yet God tells Jeremiah that Israel does just that. They had tried to dig their own leaky cisterns and were looking for water there instead of at the water's source. How foolish! How regrettable!

Through the prophet Jeremiah, God condemned his people for turning away from him, "the fountain of living water." Living water meant a bubbling spring or a flowing river—pure and life-giving. What a clear picture of what people actually lose when they turn away from God!

People today still choose other ways to try to quench their spiritual thirst. We dig cisterns of materialism, relationships, popularity, power, and so forth. Ultimately, those cisterns leak, and their contents do not satisfy. But God's life-giving stream still flows nearby, available and free.

Sip to take away

Are you thirsty for fulfillment? Your thirst is genuine, but it needs to be quenched from a genuine source. Drink from God's stream!

a cup of . . .

God's Holiness

LIVING WATER

No one is holy like the LORD!
   There is no one besides you;
   there is no Rock like our God.   1 SAMUEL 2:2

Who is God except the LORD?
   Who but our God is a solid rock?   PSALM 18:31

You are holy.
   The praises of Israel surround your throne.

PSALM 22:3

Thirst-quenching thought for the day

The book of 1 Samuel begins with a desperate woman. Hannah needed a miracle. Desperately wanting a child, she prayed and asked God to give her a son. In return, she vowed she would dedicate the child to the Lord and to his service. God answered Hannah's request, and Hannah kept her promise. The words in the first passage above are from her dedication prayer.

Hannah prayed with joy and gratitude. She was thrilled with her new situation—the mother of a miracle child—yet she rejoiced not in what had happened to her but in who God was. Notice that Hannah's prayer highlights God's holiness, proclaiming that no one like God exists; in fact, no one is even close.

Next, Hannah exclaimed that God stood as the greatest "Rock." This pictures God as solid and secure, but it also implies safety. Hannah knew God to be rock solid, a secure haven for her soul.

Sip to take away

When you feel desperate and hope for a miracle, to whom do you turn? Do you acknowledge that the Lord alone is holy—that he is the only one who can answer your request?

a cup of...
God's Patience

LIVING WATER

*These things I plan won't happen right away.
Slowly, steadily, surely, the time approaches when
the vision will be fulfilled. If it seems slow, wait
patiently, for it will surely take place. It will not be
delayed.*   HABAKKUK 2:3

*Don't you realize how kind, tolerant, and patient
God is with you? Or don't you care? Can't you see
how kind he has been in giving you time to turn
from your sin?*   ROMANS 2:4

*The Lord isn't really being slow about his promise
to return, as some people think. No, he is being
patient for your sake. He does not want anyone to
perish, so he is giving more time for everyone to
repent.*   2 PETER 3:9

Thirst-quenching
thought for the day

The first-century believers who read Peter's letter were enduring persecution. They must have wondered often why God would allow them to suffer so much and why Jesus had not yet returned to rescue his own people, to judge evil, to right wrongs, and to punish evildoers. Habakkuk's words remind us that God's people have long felt this way.

We may have the same questions today, especially when we see blatant disregard for God, callous disobedience of God's laws, and much suffering for the faith. These verses give the answer—God's patience.

God will accomplish his plans. Jesus will return. God will punish those determined to live apart from him. Perfect justice will reign. But not yet, because God is waiting, giving more and more people the opportunity to turn from their sins and to turn to him.

Sip to take away

Whenever you wonder why God doesn't suddenly appear and eliminate all sin and suffering, think of his loving patience. And remember that he was patient with you, giving you time to hear the gospel, to repent, and to trust in Christ as your Savior.

a cup of . . .
God's Persistence

LIVING WATER

Surely your goodness and unfailing love will
*   pursue me*
*   all the days of my life,*
and I will live in the house of the LORD forever.

PSALM 23:6

Remember, O LORD, your unfailing love and
*   compassion,*
*   which you have shown from long ages past.*
Forgive the rebellious sins of my youth;
*   look instead through the eyes of your unfailing*
*   love,*
*   for you are merciful, O LORD.*
The LORD is good and does what is right;
*   he shows the proper path to those who go astray.*
He leads the humble in what is right,
*   teaching them his way.*
The LORD leads with unfailing love and faithfulness
*   all those who keep his covenant and obey his*
*   decrees.*

PSALM 25:6-10

Thirst-quenching
thought for the day

Apparently, David discovered that looking back over life can be worthwhile, as long as we are looking for the right things. He understood the way God pursues us. David is saying in Psalm 23 that God's goodness and love will chase after him, aggressively following him "all the days" of his life.

Like David, our purpose should be to spot evidence in our life of God's goodness and love just behind us.

What a beautiful picture and encouraging promise for those who belong to the Lord—we can never outrun his love, and he runs right behind us every step of the way. This means that

- If everyone deserts us, God will be with us.
- Wherever we are and whatever we are going through, God's love will be there.
- Regardless of the evil in the world, God's goodness will come through.

And the ultimate goal of God pursuing us with his goodness and love is life with our Lord, forever!

Sip to take away

If you lose sight of God while running through a hectic and pressure-packed life, turn around—he is there.

a cup of . . .

God's Presence

LIVING WATER

No one will be able to stand their ground against you as long as you live. For I will be with you as I was with Moses. I will not fail you or abandon you.

JOSHUA 1:5

The LORD is for me, so I will not be afraid.
  What can mere mortals do to me?
Yes, the LORD is for me; he will help me.
  I will look in triumph at those who hate me.
It is better to trust the LORD
  than to put confidence in people.   PSALM 118:6-8

Thirst-quenching
thought for the day

Poised to assume the leadership of God's people, Joshua must have wondered if he was up to such an awesome task. Besides the great responsibility of being the political and military leader, Joshua also served as spiritual leader. His job was to lead God's people into the Promised Land, to keep them focused on the Lord as they settled the land and organized as a nation.

Joshua also knew the great price of leadership—loneliness. He alone stood as the leader; no one else could take credit for success or blame for failure.

At this critical time of transition, God spoke to Joshua, assuring him of his presence and power. And God's word to his man has echoed through time as a word of assurance to all of his people: "I will not fail you or abandon you." (See also Deuteronomy 31:6; 31:8; Hebrews 13:5.)

Sip to take away

God has called you to leadership—in your home, on the job, in the community, or at church. As you plan, organize, and motivate, know that you don't lead alone— God stands with you. And when those lonely times come, know that you are not alone— God will never leave you.

a cup of . . .

God's Requirements

LIVING WATER

Now, Israel, what does the LORD your God require of you? He requires you to fear him, to live according to his will, to love and worship him with all your heart and soul, and to obey the Lord's commands and laws that I am giving you today for your own good.

DEUTERONOMY 10:12-13

No, O people, the LORD has already told you what is good, and this is what he requires: to do what is right, to love mercy, and to walk humbly with your God.

MICAH 6:8

Pay all your debts, except the debt of love for others. You can never finish paying that! If you love your neighbor, you will fulfill all the requirements of God's law.

ROMANS 13:8

Thirst-quenching
thought for the day

At times, you may wonder what God expects. The flood of messages and instructions from others, combined with those from yourself, can be overwhelming. But the prophet Micah summarized it well: 1) Do what is right, 2) love mercy, 3) walk humbly.

Justice. Mercy. Humility. Consider what kind of life these qualities would lead to if you put them into practice. How would your life change? What would be their impact on your relationships? What would your community and nation be like if citizens lived according to this pattern? Most importantly, what would happen in your relationship with God?

Micah ties these three things together—justice, mercy, and walking with God. When we love justice and mercy, we will be walking humbly with God; and likewise, walking humbly with God we will love justice and mercy and live them out in our daily lives.

Sip to take away

Which of the three qualities Micah mentioned most clearly invites your attention today? Ask God to supply your need for justice and mercy. Then live this day in humble dependence on him.

a cup of...

God's Spirit

LIVING WATER

I will send you the Counselor —the Spirit of truth. He will come to you from the Father and will tell you all about me. JOHN 15:26

When the Holy Spirit controls our lives, he will produce this kind of fruit in us: love, joy, peace, patience, kindness, goodness, faithfulness, gentleness, and self-control. Here there is no conflict with the law. GALATIANS 5:22-23

God has not given us a spirit of fear and timidity, but of power, love, and self-discipline. 2 TIMOTHY 1:7

Thirst-quenching
thought for the day

In John 15:26, Jesus is teaching the disciples about the Holy Spirit, the "Spirit of truth." Translated as "Counselor," the Greek word literally means "one who comes alongside." So this title pictures one person coming alongside to guide (as would occur on a path in the woods), to advise (as with a lawyer in a court of law), to counsel (as in a pastor's office or between trusted friends), to speak words of concern and love (as with loved ones in a hospital room), or to comfort (as at a graveside).

Clearly, God sends his Spirit to help all believers, his children whom he loves dearly. And he counsels and comforts them by telling the truth about Jesus. He also creates in their lives the "fruit," or character traits, of Jesus listed in Galatians 5 above. The needs and hurts of life simply provide a clear opportunity to experience the ministry of God's Spirit.

Sip to take away
Do you feel lost, wondering which way to turn? Are you devastated by loss and overcome with grief? The Comforter is close, wrapping his arms around you and whispering words of love.

a cup of . . .

God's Unfailing Love

LIVING WATER

The LORD did not choose you and lavish his love on you because you were larger or greater than other nations, for you were the smallest of all nations! It was simply because the LORD loves you, and because he was keeping the oath he had sworn to your ancestors. DEUTERONOMY 7:7-8

*Remember, O LORD, your unfailing love and
    compassion,
  which you have shown from long ages past.
Forgive the rebellious sins of my youth;
  look instead through the eyes of your
      unfailing love,
  for you are merciful, O LORD.* PSALM 25:6-7

Long ago the LORD said to Israel: "I have loved you, my people, with an everlasting love. With unfailing love I have drawn you to myself." JEREMIAH 31:3

Thirst-quenching thought for the day

As a child, walking into your grandparents' home, you would be met with open arms and the familiar greeting, "Come and give grandma a hug!" That's the picture here: God opening his arms and welcoming his children—drawing them to himself with kindness and love. What an unforgettable welcome!

In Israel's case, these statements of love and restoration come after dark prophetic predictions of God punishing his people, allowing them to be conquered and captured. Certainly they deserved it; actually, they deserved even more. They had rejected God, worshiping idols instead, and had refused to listen to God's warnings through his prophets. So they would be punished.

But God's punishment is always tempered with mercy because of his great love, described here as "everlasting" and "unfailing."

Sip to take away

The message is clear: No matter what you have done, God still loves you. As in the past, so in the present—he waits with open arms, drawing you with loving-kindness. Turn from your idols to the living God. Turn from your sin and indifference and run to the Savior.

a cup of...

Good Things

Living Water

Praise the LORD, I tell myself;
  with my whole heart, I will praise his holy name.
Praise the LORD, I tell myself,
  and never forget the good things he does for me.
He forgives all my sins
  and heals all my diseases.
He ransoms me from death
  and surrounds me with love and tender mercies.
He fills my life with good things.
  My youth is renewed like the eagle's!   Psalm 103:1-5

You have done many good things for me, LORD,
  just as you promised.   Psalm 119:65

Thirst-quenching thought for the day

Each year we have Thanksgiving, a holiday set aside for remembering and counting all our blessings.

In Psalm 103 David, inspired by God's Spirit, proclaims his gratitude to God for all his "good things." Clearly this is a song of thanksgiving—David praising his wonderful Lord for who he is and for all his mighty works.

Consider some of the benefits listed in light of what you are experiencing:

- Forgives all your sins: Regardless of what you have done, God forgives through Christ Jesus your Lord.

- Heals all your diseases: God brings you through the tough times and the pain.

- Ransoms you from death: When you were sinking in sin, utterly without hope, God pulled you up and set your feet on solid ground. You have been rescued, redeemed, saved!

Sip to take away

Now it's your turn to give God conscious praise for his gift of good things in your life!

a cup of . . .

Gratitude

LIVING WATER

Praise the Lord; praise God our savior!
  For each day he carries us in his arms. . . .

Sing to God, you kingdoms of the earth.
  Sing praises to the Lord.
Sing to the one who rides across the ancient
    heavens,
  his mighty voice thundering from the sky.
Tell everyone about God's power.
  His majesty shines down on Israel;
  his strength is mighty in the heavens.
God is awesome in his sanctuary.
  The God of Israel gives power and strength to his
    people.

Praise be to God!   PSALM 68:19, 32-35

Thirst-quenching thought for the day

The psalms of David overflow with praise. Having seen God work in his life—rescuing, protecting, guiding, strengthening, and forgiving—David the musician-king often wrote and sang of his deep gratitude to his loving Lord.

This song of David praises God as the one who has faithfully carried his people. The psalm expresses a confident hope in God's future help, which flows out of a knowledge of God's help in the past.

Note that David emphasizes that God bears his people each day. In other words, God doesn't take one load and then move on to something else. He carries his people daily in his arms. The phrase implies intimacy as well as power. The song goes on to list powerful ways in which God handles enemies. It expresses, in vivid terms, a rhetorical question asked by the Apostle Paul, "If God is for us, who can ever be against us?" (Romans 8:31). God's faithfulness offers us a continual reminder to express gratitude.

Sip to take away

What weighs you down? Thank God you have a burden-bearer. He carries both you and your burdens every day.

a cup of . . .

Guidance

LIVING WATER

The LORD says, "I will guide you along the best
pathway for your life.
I will advise you and watch over you."   PSALM 32:8

The LORD watches over those who fear him,
those who rely on his unfailing love.
He rescues them from death
and keeps them alive in times of famine.

PSALM 33:18-19

Trust in the LORD with all your heart; do not depend
on your own understanding. Seek his will in all you
do, and he will direct your paths.   PROVERBS 3:5-6

Thirst-quenching thought for the day

Children think they know just about everything. One junior high student recently remarked that he didn't need to go to church because he "knew all the stories." Adolescents are known for their cocky self-assuredness.

The older we get, however, the more we realize how little knowledge we actually possess. We find that we have more and more questions and fewer and fewer answers. Life often seems gray, rather than black and white. We struggle with complex issues, problems with no obvious solutions. We wonder what to do, which way to turn, how to live, and where to go. And we often begin to doubt.

But God's promises in these verses give us hope. Note that he doesn't offer simple solutions and easy answers; he offers himself. God says he will guide, advise, and direct. In other words, God will help us go in the right direction and then watch over us along the road.

Sip to take away

What life-issues boggle your mind? What decisions slow you down? What problems harass your steps? Look to the Lord for guidance. You can rely on him. He won't zap you to your destination, but he will guide you along the way.

a cup of . . .

Hard Work

LIVING WATER

Never be lazy in your work, but serve the Lord enthusiastically.   ROMANS 12:11

Work hard and cheerfully at whatever you do, as though you were working for the Lord rather than for people. Remember that the Lord will give you an inheritance as your reward, and the Master you are serving is Christ.   COLOSSIANS 3:23-24

Work hard so God can approve you. Be a good worker, one who does not need to be ashamed and who correctly explains the word of truth.

2 TIMOTHY 2:15

Thirst-quenching thought for the day

"No one appreciates me!" Have you ever felt that way? Working hard behind the scenes, almost anonymously, you feel overlooked, neglected, taken for granted.

Employers make mistakes. Bosses become bossy. Supervisors reward incompetence. Teachers fail. Managers mismanage. All of those things come with living in a sinful world with fallible, sinful human beings.

Regardless of our situation, however, we need to work as though we are working for God, rather than for our earthly employer. God knows what's going on—both with us and with our employer. He sees our work and knows the attitude with which we do it.

Understanding whom we serve should motivate us to work hard and to be honest in all our dealings. It also frees us from the trap of seeking earthly rewards and acclaim. No amount of money can match God's "inheritance," and no accolades can compare with God's "Well done!" that awaits all who trust Christ and serve him.

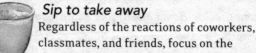

Sip to take away

Regardless of the reactions of coworkers, classmates, and friends, focus on the Lord and work for him. His pay is worth living for.

a cup of . . .
Honoring God

LIVING WATER

How can a young person stay pure?
   By obeying your word and following its rules.
I have tried my best to find you—
   don't let me wander from your commands.
I have hidden your word in my heart,
   that I might not sin against you.   PSALM 119:9-11

Then you will understand what it means to fear the LORD, and you will gain knowledge of God. For the LORD grants wisdom! From his mouth come knowledge and understanding.   PROVERBS 2:5-6

Don't let the excitement of youth cause you to forget your Creator. Honor him in your youth before you grow old and no longer enjoy living.   ECCLESIASTES 12:1

Thirst-quenching thought for the day

It's wonderful to be young and filled with optimism, promise, and potential. But youthful excitement can deaden common sense and distort vision. Too often, while focusing on the present and on good feelings, they can forget God, the One who created them and loves them and who can guide them through what lies ahead.

Suddenly, the future is now, and individuals begin to struggle with the realities of life as an adult. Then those who have built on shaky foundations see and feel their lives beginning to crumble. The hard lesson learned by each generation is that a life begun without God leads to a life lived without God, which leads to a life ending in pain and bitterness without God.

In contrast, those who honor God while they are young focus their lives on doing his will—living the way he desires. Then, when nearing the end, they look forward with hope to a glorious eternity with their Savior.

Sip to take away

Clearly, these passages teach that regardless of your standing—age, maturity, experience, expertise—God needs to be the center of your life. Remember him and live fully.

a cup of . . .
Insight

LIVING WATER

Cry out for insight and understanding. Search for them as you would for lost money or hidden treasure.   PROVERBS 2:3-4

Keep on asking, and you will be given what you ask for. Keep on looking, and you will find. Keep on knocking, and the door will be opened. For everyone who asks, receives. Everyone who seeks, finds. And the door is opened to everyone who knocks.

MATTHEW 7:7-8

If you need wisdom—if you want to know what God wants you to do—ask him, and he will gladly tell you. He will not resent your asking. But when you ask him, be sure that you really expect him to answer, for a doubtful mind is as unsettled as a wave of the sea that is driven and tossed by the wind.   JAMES 1:5-6

Thirst-quenching thought for the day

Doubts assail like gale-force winds, tossing us this way and that. We wonder what to do, which way to turn, which direction to travel. We may even question our faith, doubting God's goodness or even that he is there. Like night storms, difficult circumstances can terrify us, confuse us, and fill us with anxiety. But God's truth cuts through the darkness like a powerful beam from a lighthouse, providing warning, direction, security, and hope. We aren't abandoned to our doubts and uncertainties. God says we can ask him, and he will answer "gladly."

We may be tempted to give up when confronted with what seem like unanswerable questions, but these passages remind us that we must turn away from what creates doubt and toward what affirms faith. God provides that in himself and his Word.

Sip to take away

Do you want to know what to do? Do you desire to follow God's way? Do you need assurance of his presence and love? Ask God for insight into his will. He will answer.

a cup of . . .

Joy

LIVING WATER

You have turned my mourning into joyful dancing.
*   You have taken away my clothes of mourning and*
*   clothed me with joy,*   PSALM 30:11

Those who have been ransomed by the LORD will
return to Jerusalem, singing songs of everlasting
joy. Sorrow and mourning will disappear, and they
will be overcome with joy and gladness.   ISAIAH 51:11

The young women will dance for joy, and the
men—old and young—will join in the celebration. I
will turn their mourning into joy. I will comfort
them and exchange their sorrow for rejoicing.

                                    JEREMIAH 31:13

Thirst-quenching
thought for the day

Have you ever danced at a funeral? That would be unthinkable, absurd. Funerals are times of reflection, sorrow, and mourning. We expect funerals to bring sadness and tears, not joy and celebration.

We mourn for many reasons, and each painful loss tears our emotions and causes us to regret past actions and missed opportunities, to wonder what might have been. Certainly nothing hurts more than the death of a loved one—we miss our fiancé or spouse or child or parent or friend, and we long to hear that familiar voice and feel the person's touch.

Through the Scriptures, however, we learn that, one day, God will turn mourning into gladness and sadness into joy. That is God's plan. Because we know him, our ultimate destiny is heaven, and we have the solid assurance that one day all sickness, death, and sorrow will be banished—we will be perfect and complete. All of this earth, including our pain, is temporary, but our joy will last forever.

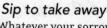

Sip to take away
Whatever your sorrow, keep your eyes on Christ and maintain an eternal perspective. Look forward to the day when we all will sing and dance with joy again!

a cup of . . .
Liberation

LIVING WATER

In fact, we expected to die. But as a result, we learned not to rely on ourselves, but on God who can raise the dead. And he did deliver us from mortal danger. And we are confident that he will continue to deliver us.
2 CORINTHIANS 1:9-10

The Lord stood with me and gave me strength, that I might preach the Good News in all its fullness for all the Gentiles to hear. And he saved me from certain death. Yes, and the Lord will deliver me from every evil attack and will bring me safely to his heavenly Kingdom. To God be the glory forever and ever. Amen.
2 TIMOTHY 4:17-18

Thirst-quenching thought for the day

On his missionary journeys, Paul often found himself in desperate situations in which there seemed to be no hope. Reflecting back on one of those occasions, Paul could see that, through the hardship, God was teaching him and his traveling companions a valuable lesson: They were to rely on God and his power, not on themselves. Certainly the almighty God "who can raise the dead" could be counted upon to liberate them from both prison and "mortal danger."

Whatever the situation, Paul could place his faith in God because he knew who God was and because he had seen God work. Thus, he set his hope squarely on his awesome Lord and Savior.

Through Paul's words, we can learn what he had to learn the hard way—to rely on God.

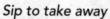

Sip to take away

What desperate circumstances confront you today? A doctor's negative report? Lack of resources? A broken relationship? Recall those special times when God rescued you in the past, and know that he can and will do it again.

a cup of . . .
Longing

LIVING WATER

O God, you are my God;
*   I earnestly search for you.*
My soul thirsts for you;
*   my whole body longs for you*
in this parched and weary land
*   where there is no water.*   PSALM 63:1

I reach out for you.
*   I thirst for you as parched land thirsts for rain.*

Come quickly, LORD, and answer me,
*   for my depression deepens.*
Don't turn away from me,
*   or I will die.*
Let me hear of your unfailing love to me in the
*   morning,*
*   for I am trusting you.*
Show me where to walk,
*   for I have come to you in prayer.*   PSALM 143:6-8

Thirst-quenching thought for the day

The psalm writers honestly expressed themselves to God—every feeling from elation to despair. While fighting anxiety, depression, and fear, these strugglers turned to God. Remembering the Lord's mighty works of the past, they prayed for a miracle in the present. They longed for God to make himself known to them again.

Believers today experience the whole range of emotional ups and downs. The emotions themselves are not wrong or sinful; they just are. But our response is critical. We can allow our emotions to pull us away from God or to push us toward him. In the case recorded in Psalm 143, the writer's depression moved him in God's direction. First, he acknowledged his need and his total dependence on God. Then he asked for God's guidance. When we choose to do the same, God responds to us, just as he did the psalmists long ago.

Sip to take away

Don't allow fear and depression to drive you from the Lord. Instead, tell him how you feel and ask for his help.

a cup of . . .

Love

LIVING WATER

I am convinced that nothing can ever separate us from his love. Death can't, and life can't. The angels can't, and the demons can't. Our fears for today, our worries about tomorrow, and even the powers of hell can't keep God's love away. ROMANS 8:38

May you have the power to understand, as all God's people should, how wide, how long, how high, and how deep his love really is. May you experience the love of Christ, though it is so great you will never fully understand it. Then you will be filled with the fullness of life and power that comes from God.
EPHESIANS 3:18-19

But I am not ashamed of [preaching the gospel], for I know the one in whom I trust, and I am sure that he is able to guard what I have entrusted to him until the day of his return. 2 TIMOTHY 1:12

Thirst-quenching thought for the day

Writing from prison, Paul declared to Timothy his confidence in Christ. He was not ashamed of his situation or his Lord and, despite his suffering, he continued to boldly proclaim his faith. Although Paul knew that he probably would be executed soon, he stood strong. Paul was convinced of the truth of the gospel and of the strength and faithfulness of the love of his Lord and Savior. He knew the one in whose hands he had placed his present and his future, and he knew he was held in God's love.

Although not facing martyrdom in a Roman dungeon, you still may feel imprisoned and under assault, with no hope of rescue or release. That's when you need to refocus your attention on the truth of God's love, remembering the one in whom you believed.

Sip to take away

Today, review and renew your trust in God's love for you. He is with you, and nothing can ever separate you from his love.

a cup of . . .
Mercy

LIVING WATER

Where is another God like you, who pardons the sins of the survivors among his people? You cannot stay angry with your people forever, because you delight in showing mercy.   MICAH 7:18

God is so rich in mercy, and he loved us so very much.   EPHESIANS 2:4

He saved us, not because of the good things we did, but because of his mercy. He washed away our sins and gave us a new life through the Holy Spirit.

TITUS 3:5

Thirst-quenching thought for the day

God can certainly be seen through different lenses. One lens reveals God as judge and emphasizes his anger; as the righteous Sovereign, he judges sin and punishes sinners. Certainly this picture is true; God does reign supremely and justly. We should fear his wrath and obey his commands. These verses, however, emphasize that although God lives forever, he does not stay angry that long. In fact, God delights to show mercy. In this view, God is like a loving father with a disobedient child. Knowing that he must punish, he would much rather have the child repent so that he can also show mercy and forgive.

The word *survivors* refers to God's people, Israel, who in spite of severe judgments were never wiped out. God preserved them. Their experiences remind us that God protects and preserves even through punishment. Sometimes we don't realize how badly we need God's mercy until we are suffering the results of sin.

Sip to take away

Hear the lesson, child of God. Your Father loves you and stands ready to pardon your sin. Don't be afraid. Don't run away in fear. Confess your sin and receive his mercy.

a cup of . . .

Patience

LIVING WATER

Wait patiently for the LORD.
   Be brave and courageous.
   Yes, wait patiently for the LORD.   PSALM 27:14

Don't be impatient for the LORD to act!
   Travel steadily along his path.
He will honor you, giving you the land.
   You will see the wicked destroyed.   PSALM 37:34

Those who wait on the LORD will find new strength.
They will fly high on wings like eagles. They will run
and not grow weary. They will walk and not faint.
                                        ISAIAH 40:31

Thirst-quenching thought for the day

Waiting is difficult in a hurried, fast-paced world. Waiting is frustrating for impatient people. We want answers and service and money and success and healing, and we want them now! But God calls us to be patient, to wait for him and his timing.

That only makes sense, of course. God knows us, he knows the future, and his timing is perfect. Of course we should wait. Of course we should endure. Of course we should listen for his voice and follow his guidance.

But instead, we rush headlong into life. Then we wonder why we struggle and fear. Waiting for the Lord means recognizing his wisdom, acknowledging his sovereignty, and submitting to his control. Waiting involves prayer, talking to God about our dilemmas and decisions, and pouring out our feelings. As we wait, God gives us strength and courage to meet the challenges before us.

Sip to take away

Looking for a quick fix? Immediate gratification? Easy answers? Instead, wait for the Lord.

a cup of . . .

Peace

LIVING WATER

I lay down and slept.
  I woke up in safety,
  for the LORD was watching over me.
I am not afraid of ten thousand enemies
  who surround me on every side.   PSALM 3:5-6

I will lie down in peace and sleep,
  for you alone, O LORD, will keep me safe.   PSALM 4:8

I know the LORD is always with me.
  I will not be shaken, for he is right beside me.
No wonder my heart is filled with joy,
  and my mouth shouts his praises!
  My body rests in safety.   PSALM 16:8-9

Thirst-quenching thought for the day

For months, David was harassed in the palace and then chased through the desert by King Saul. Later, during his own reign as king, David faced a host of enemies from outside Israel's borders and from within. Eventually even two of his own sons, Absalom and Adonijah, tried to overthrow him. David must have feared for his safety as he encountered enemies at every turn.

But David lived confidently, secure in his relationship with his loving heavenly Father. In this song David writes that he could "lie down in peace and sleep" because God protected him.

Like David, you may be surrounded by enemies who are intent on causing you great harm. Perhaps even loved ones have turned against you. Sleep has not come quickly at night, with anxieties and fears filling your dreams. You may even fear for your life.

If so, check out David's secret for sleeping "in peace." The secret? David focused his attention on the Lord instead of the situation, remembering God's power and love. And he prayed about his situation and his worries (Psalm 4:1).

Sip to take away
Lie down in peace and sleep, since God keeps you safe.

a cup of . . .

Perception

LIVING WATER

Do not be afraid that some plan conceived behind closed doors will be the end of you. Do not fear anything except the LORD Almighty. He alone is the Holy One. If you fear him, you need fear nothing else.　　　　　ISAIAH 8:12-13

Don't be afraid of those who want to kill you. They can only kill your body; they cannot touch your soul. Fear only God, who can destroy both soul and body in hell. Not even a sparrow, worth only half a penny, can fall to the ground without your Father knowing it. And the very hairs on your head are all numbered. So don't be afraid; you are more valuable to him than a whole flock of sparrows.　　　　　MATTHEW 10:28-31

Jesus knew what they were thinking, so he said, "You have so little faith! Why are you worried about having no food?"　　　　　MATTHEW 16:8

Thirst-quenching
thought for the day

A sparrow is one of the smallest birds and surely one of the most common and ordinary. Sparrows come in many varieties and can be found all over the world.

In Matthew 10, Jesus used this tiny and seemingly insignificant creature to illustrate God's care for the earth and to teach the value of God's highest creation—human beings. How much are sparrows worth? In the world, not very much. But God knows when each one falls. How much more are you worth according to the world? according to God?

Living in a world that almost daily announces a de-valuing of persons, we need to hear Christ's words. We are precious to him, down to our numbered hairs—even when those numbers decrease daily!

Sip to take away
Whenever you feel hopeless, helpless, or worthless, consider that you are valuable to God. He knows you, watches over you, and cares for you.

a cup of . . .

Perspective

LIVING WATER

Have you never heard or understood? Are you deaf to the words of God—the words he gave before the world began? Are you so ignorant? It is God who sits above the circle of the earth. The people below must seem to him like grasshoppers! He is the one who spreads out the heavens like a curtain and makes his tent from them. He judges the great people of the world and brings them all to nothing. ISAIAH 40:21-23

You have forgotten the LORD, your Creator, the one who put the stars in the sky and established the earth. Will you remain in constant dread of human oppression? Will you continue to fear the anger of your enemies from morning till night? ISAIAH 51:13

Thirst-quenching
thought for the day

- A coup topples a government. The new dictator jails all who oppose his rule.

- A revered leader dies. His son succeeds and vows to rule the nation with an iron hand.

- A bloody civil war tears a country along ethnic lines, with leaders of both sides mourning their dead and vowing revenge.

- An election sweeps a new party into power. The president-elect boasts of a mandate and promises broad reforms.

With our eyes firmly fixed on this world, we may feel impotent in the face of military might, political power, and majority rule. Yet Isaiah reminds us that only God, our Creator and Redeemer, truly reigns. His power knows no limit; he is sovereign and in control. Despite the ranting and raving of earthly leaders, they are ultimately subject to God's rule. One day they will be reduced to nothing.

Sip to take away

Regardless of the political winds, keep your allegiance and attention on your sovereign Lord. He will bring you through.

a cup of . . .

Possibility

LIVING WATER

The LORD said to Abraham, "Why did Sarah laugh? Why did she say, 'Can an old woman like me have a baby?' Is anything too hard for the LORD? About a year from now, just as I told you, I will return, and Sarah will have a son."   GENESIS 18:13-14

O Sovereign LORD! You have made the heavens and earth by your great power. Nothing is too hard for you!   JEREMIAH 32:17

I can do everything with the help of Christ who gives me the strength I need.   PHILIPPIANS 4:13

Thirst-quenching thought for the day

At nearly a hundred years old, Abraham and Sarah were astounded at God's announcement that they would have a son. Decades beyond child-bearing years, Sarah chuckled at the prospect, thinking the promise impossible to fulfill. So God had to remind them that nothing was too difficult for him. And true to God's word, Isaac ("laughter") was born one year later.

Two great truths emerge from this incident:

- God can do anything—nothing is too hard for the Lord.
- God keeps his promises.

Both the prophet Jeremiah and the apostle Paul understood that God makes hard things possible. Their lives were examples of that truth!

Sip to take away
What "too hard" task do you face? If God wants you to do it, you can, if you do it with him—"with God all things are possible" (Matthew 19:26).

a cup of . . .

Power

LIVING WATER

Now glory be to God! By his mighty power at work within us, he is able to accomplish infinitely more than we would ever dare to ask or hope. May he be given glory in the church and in Christ Jesus forever and ever through endless ages. Amen.

EPHESIANS 3:20-21

I can do everything with the help of Christ who gives me the strength I need. PHILIPPIANS 4:13

As we know Jesus better, his divine power gives us everything we need for living a godly life. He has called us to receive his own glory and goodness! And by that same mighty power, he has given us all of his rich and wonderful promises. He has promised that you will escape the decadence all around you caused by evil desires and that you will share in his divine nature. 2 PETER 1:3-4

Thirst-quenching thought for the day

How easily we forget our powerlessness! We think we have life all figured out, under control. Confident of the possibilities, we predict what will happen in the days, months, and years ahead.

Then suddenly, we are caught off guard as reality hits. Surprised by circumstances—diagnosed illness, natural disaster, a torn relationship—we become painfully aware of our mortality and finiteness. Then we realize that we actually have no real control and can only guess at what is to come.

But God knows the future and the past, and he knows us perfectly. He knows what we need and what will bring us joy. Think of it: We can't imagine the fantastic future that God has prepared for us. We can't even come close in our asking. His plans reach far beyond our wildest dreams.

Sip to take away

When blindsided by life, look up and hope. God's power works within you, and he is working for you, more than you can imagine.

a cup of . . .
Preparation

LIVING WATER

Be prepared, because you don't know what day your Lord is coming. MATTHEW 24:42

You aren't in the dark about these things, dear brothers and sisters, and you won't be surprised when the day of the Lord comes like a thief. For you are all children of the light and of the day; we don't belong to darkness and night. So be on your guard, not asleep like the others. Stay alert and be sober.

1 THESSALONIANS 5:4-6

It was not long after he said this that he was taken up into the sky while they were watching, and he disappeared into a cloud. As they were straining their eyes to see him, two white-robed men suddenly stood there among them. They said, "Men of Galilee, why are you standing here staring at the sky? Jesus has been taken away from you into heaven. And someday, just as you saw him go, he will return!"

ACTS 1:9-11

Thirst-quenching thought for the day

Why did the disciples stand and look intently into the sky? Maybe they were stunned and amazed at seeing Jesus ascend into the air through the clouds. Maybe they were saddened by his sudden disappearance and were looking anxiously for him to descend again. Or perhaps they were confused and didn't know what else to do.

Whatever the disciples' thoughts or motives were, two angels ("men in white") gave them the word. They could stop looking up and start looking around at the world and its needy people (John 4:35). They could stop wondering and start working to fulfill Christ's commission (Matthew 28:18-20), living with the assurance that Jesus would come again, just as he had promised (John 14:3).

Although some two thousand years have passed since this dramatic event, the angels' message still stands—Jesus will surely return. That truth should continue to motivate believers as we work for Christ and his kingdom.

Sip to take away

Keep hoping, working, loving, sharing the Good News, and living for the Savior. He will come back, and we need to be prepared for that day.

a cup of . . .

Promises

LIVING WATER

The LORD's promises are pure,
  like silver refined in a furnace,
  purified seven times over.   PSALM 12:6

As for God, his way is perfect.
  All the LORD's promises prove true.
  He is a shield for all who look to him for
    protection.   PSALM 18:30

He will shield you with his wings.
  He will shelter you with his feathers.
  His faithful promises are your armor and
    protection.   PSALM 91:4

Thirst-quenching
thought for the day

In describing the Lord and his promises, Psalm 91 gives two vivid metaphors for God's protection. The first is a mother hen sheltering her chicks from a storm. The second is a strong and sturdy shield protecting a soldier in battle.

Both word pictures describe a God whose promises can be counted on in our time of deepest need. At times, we need shelter, refuge from the wind and rain of life. In the shelter we live in safety—warm, dry, and secure.

At other times we need a shield to protect us from the attacks of those who would harm us: human enemies and spiritual forces, hateful and evil.

God provides our refuge—his promises. And he provides the shield—his faithfulness. He promised!

Sip to take away

When threats arise, seek shelter in the Lord. In your battles, trust in the shield of God's promises.

a cup of . . .

Provision

LIVING WATER

The LORD is my shepherd;
*   I have everything I need.*
He lets me rest in green meadows;
*   he leads me beside peaceful streams.*
*   He renews my strength.*
He guides me along right paths,
*   bringing honor to his name.*   PSALM 23:1-3

God will generously provide all you need. Then you
will always have everything you need and plenty
left over to share with others.   2 CORINTHIANS 9:8

This same God who takes care of me will supply all
your needs from his glorious riches, which have
been given to us in Christ Jesus.   PHILIPPIANS 4:19

Thirst-quenching thought for the day

- God—holy, perfect, infinite, loving, all-powerful, all-knowing, ever present
- will—in the future it will happen; it's a promise
- supply—complete, fulfill, meet, satisfy
- all your needs—not your wants, but everything you truly need
- from his glorious riches—unlimited power and resources
- in Christ Jesus—the sinless Son sacrificed for you

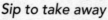

Sip to take away

Philippians 4:19 says it all. No matter how weak and desperate you feel, hold on to this verse. God has said it, and he will do it. Depend on him.

a cup of . . .
Real Living

LIVING WATER

While we live, we live to please the Lord. And when we die, we go to be with the Lord. So in life and in death, we belong to the Lord. Christ died and rose again for this very purpose, so that he might be Lord of those who are alive and of those who have died.

ROMANS 14:8-9

He died for everyone so that those who receive his new life will no longer live to please themselves. Instead, they will live to please Christ, who died and was raised for them. 2 CORINTHIANS 5:15

For to me, living is for Christ, and dying is even better. Yet if I live, that means fruitful service for Christ. I really don't know which is better.

PHILIPPIANS 1:21-22

Thirst-quenching
thought for the day

Some of the people you will meet today live in terror. They are afraid not only of dying, but also of thinking about dying. They have reached the desperate conclusion that the only way to postpone death involves not thinking about it. A person who refuses to include death's reality in their thinking finds it hard to live life fully.

Paul took death for granted. He included it in his plans. In fact, he considered himself dead already (Galatians 2:20). He faced the inevitable because he eagerly anticipated what waited beyond death. By looking past death, he could see death in its context, not as a dreaded end but as a necessary passage. As a result, Paul found the freedom to live fully.

We need to listen to God's truth shouted across the centuries—life in Christ is real living! Whether living or dead, you belong to the Lord. And to apply that assertion, Paul adds: "For to me, living is for Christ, and dying is even better."

Sip to take away

A believer faces death in the best company: Christ has already been there. In him you know that death is defeated and you will be with him on the other side. Live in that confidence.

a cup of . . .

Reconciliation

LIVING WATER

Christ himself has made peace between us Jews and you Gentiles by making us all one people. He has broken down the wall of hostility that used to separate us. . . . He has brought this Good News of peace to you Gentiles who were far away from him, and to us Jews who were near. Now all of us, both Jews and Gentiles, may come to the Father through the same Holy Spirit because of what Christ has done for us.

EPHESIANS 2:14, 17-18

God in all his fullness was pleased to live in Christ, and by him God reconciled everything to himself. He made peace with everything in heaven and on earth by means of his blood on the cross. COLOSSIANS 1:19-20

Thirst-quenching thought for the day

When the Berlin Wall came down, the world celebrated. Tyranny had been defeated; a nation and families were reunited; peace had come!

In a similar way Jesus is our "peace." He has removed the barrier separating us from God. We built that wall with our sin, our hostility toward God, and we lived in desperate darkness on the other side. But Jesus obliterated the terrible wall by paying the penalty for our sin on the cross. Before, we were at war with God; now we are at peace.

This peace knows no barriers. Gentiles "were far away," while Jews "were near." In other words, all who trust in Christ have "access to the Father," no matter what their original distance from him.

It is possible, of course, to live as though the wall still exists and miss the blessings of the Father. But how foolish! Now that the barrier is gone, don't let anything or anyone keep you from his love.

Sip to take away

Stop fighting; the war is over. The wall of sin has been torn down. Enjoy the peace that Christ has brought about.

a cup of . . .

Reflection

LIVING WATER

Give thanks to the LORD and proclaim his greatness.
Let the whole world know what he has done.
Sing to him; yes, sing his praises.
Tell everyone about his miracles.
Exult in his holy name;
O worshipers of the LORD, rejoice!
Search for the LORD and for his strength,
and keep on searching.
Think of the wonderful works he has done,
the miracles, and the judgments he handed down.

1 CHRONICLES 16:8-12

Praise the LORD, I tell myself;
with my whole heart, I will praise his holy name.
Praise the LORD, I tell myself,
and never forget the good things he does for me.

PSALM 103:1-2

Thirst-quenching thought for the day

Memory is selective. People often long for "the good old days" when, in reality, those days were no better than today. Others carry a grudge for years, bitterly clutching the memory of an insult or wrong. Some conveniently forget a past promise or commitment as they seek personal gratification. And many people forget God—who he is and what he has done.

In Psalm 103, King David urged himself as well as his people to remember the Lord—his wonders, miracles, and judgments. David's point seems to be that if we focus on the person, commandments, and works of God, we will praise him, seek him, live for him, and tell others about him. And we certainly won't despair when life gets rough.

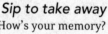

Sip to take away

How's your memory? Make a habit of thanking and praising God each day for who he is, what he has done, and what he has promised. Then tell others of his faithfulness.

a cup of . . .
Rejoicing

LIVING WATER

Then Hannah prayed:

"My heart rejoices in the LORD!
   Oh, how the LORD has blessed me!
Now I have an answer for my enemies,
   as I delight in your deliverance.
No one is holy like the LORD!
   There is no one besides you;
   there is no Rock like our God."   1 SAMUEL 2:1-2

Mary responded,

"Oh, how I praise the Lord.
   How I rejoice in God my Savior!
For he took notice of his lowly servant girl,
   and now generation after generation
   will call me blessed.
For he, the Mighty One, is holy,
   and he has done great things for me.
His mercy goes on from generation to generation,
   to all who fear him."   LUKE 1:46-50

Thirst-quenching thought for the day

The second passage above comes from Mary's inspired song of praise to God for choosing her as the one who would bear his Son. Although Mary didn't know all the details, she knew for certain that, through her, the entire world would be blessed as God fulfilled his ancient covenant with Abraham (see Genesis 15 and 17). Hannah shared a similar response, rejoicing because of God's work in her life.

Mary's song underscores two profound truths about God: He is holy, yet he also extends mercy "to all who fear him." Because of God's holiness, no sinful human being can stand in his presence; thus, all fall short of God's standard (Romans 3:23) and are cut off from him. But because of God's mercy and forgiveness, new life and eternal life are available to all who believe through Jesus, God's Son (Romans 5:8).

And because God's mercy "goes on from generation to generation," believers today can rejoice in the Lord along with Mary and Hannah.

Sip to take away
Hear this truth in Mary's song, and rejoice with her. God's mercy extends to you. Jesus came to earth, died, and rose again for you.

a cup of . . .

Rescue

LIVING WATER

He reached down from heaven and rescued me;
    he drew me out of deep waters.
He delivered me from my powerful enemies,
    from those who hated me and were too strong for
        me.
They attacked me at a moment when I was weakest,
    but the LORD upheld me.
He led me to a place of safety;
    he rescued me because he delights in me.

PSALM 18:16-19

In my distress I prayed to the LORD,
    and the LORD answered me and rescued me.

PSALM 118:5

Reach down from heaven and rescue me;
    deliver me from deep waters,
    from the power of my enemies.   PSALM 144:7

Thirst-quenching thought for the day

David sang Psalm 18 after God had rescued him from vindictive King Saul. Although David had few resources and allies, he knew that God would protect and defend him. Certainly David's enemies were too strong for him. Trying to defeat them on his own would have led to disaster. So David found his strength in almighty God, and was not disappointed.

Later, David expressed his deep gratitude to the Lord. He pictured God as reaching down from heaven, plucking him from a raging sea, and setting him on solid and dry ground. Why would God do such a thing? "Because," David answers, "he delights in me."

Few today are pursued by embittered kings and their armies. At times, however, you may feel like David, surrounded by powerful enemies. Like David, your only hope is in the Lord. Ask for his deliverance; look for his direction; depend on his strength. And after the rescue, praise his name!

Sip to take away

Ask the Lord to remind you throughout the day of this phrase: "He delights in me." Keep track of how often it makes a difference in your words and thoughts.

a cup of . . .

Resources

LIVING WATER

*Why worry about your clothes? Look at the lilies
and how they grow. They don't work or make their
clothing, yet Solomon in all his glory was not
dressed as beautifully as they are. And if God cares
so wonderfully for flowers that are here today and
gone tomorrow, won't he more surely care for you?
You have so little faith! So don't worry about having
enough food or drink or clothing.*   MATTHEW 6:28-31

*Don't worry about anything; instead, pray about
everything. Tell God what you need, and thank him
for all he has done. If you do this, you will experience God's peace, which is far more wonderful than
the human mind can understand. His peace will
guard your hearts and minds as you live in Christ
Jesus.*   PHILIPPIANS 4:6-7

*Give all your worries and cares to God, for he cares
about what happens to you.*   1 PETER 5:7

Thirst-quenching
thought for the day

Food, drink, clothes—these comprise some of the basic resources for life. Why shouldn't we worry about them? No one wants to be hungry, thirsty, or unprotected.

We must distinguish between concern and worry. Concern means being aware of specific needs and then taking steps to meet those needs. Concern leads to responsible action. It would be irresponsible and sinful, for example, for a father to be unconcerned about the basic needs of his family.

Worry, on the other hand, is concern gone to seed, an obsession with those needs. Filled with anxiety and fearing the worst, worriers nervously wonder about the future and fill their minds with ideas of the worst that could happen.

The answer to the worry question ends by understanding that God is the ultimate source of everything good and that he loves us, knows our needs, and shares our concerns.

Sip to take away
When tempted to worry about life's basic necessities, rely on this promise from Jesus: God will take care of you. As you live and work, trust him to meet your needs with his resources.

a cup of...

Resurrection

LIVING WATER

*All creation anticipates the day when it will join
God's children in glorious freedom from death and
decay.... Now that we are saved, we eagerly look
forward to this freedom. For if you already have
something, you don't need to hope for it. But if we
look forward to something we don't have yet, we
must wait patiently and confidently.*

ROMANS 8:21, 24-25

*Because God's children are human beings—made of
flesh and blood—Jesus also became flesh and blood
by being born in human form. For only as a human
being could he die, and only by dying could he break
the power of the Devil, who had the power of death.
Only in this way could he deliver those who have
lived all their lives as slaves to the fear of dying.*

HEBREWS 2:14-15

Thirst-quenching thought for the day

It's always there, lurking beneath the surface. Fear. We fear for our own well-being and for the well-being of those we love. This fear—especially the fear of death—can paralyze us. That's what motivates many to exercise endlessly and to consume all sorts of vitamins in an almost desperate attempt to postpone the inevitable.

The truth, however, is that each day our mortal, flesh-and-blood humanity steals more of our youthful beauty and vigor and moves us toward the end. Ultimately all of us will die, unless we are among the very few who will still be living when Christ returns.

Those who follow Christ also die, but they don't die forever. They live again through the power of their risen and triumphant Lord. When Jesus died on the cross, he took the death penalty for all who trust in him. And when Jesus rose from the grave, he conquered that fearful enemy. His resurrection holds the promise that we also will rise.

Sip to take away

Don't be a slave to fear. Christ has set you free by destroying the power of death. Live with the joyful knowledge that you have eternal life.

a cup of...

Riches

LIVING WATER

Don't store up treasures here on earth, where they can be eaten by moths and get rusty, and where thieves break in and steal. Store your treasures in heaven, where they will never become moth-eaten or rusty and where they will be safe from thieves. Wherever your treasure is, there your heart and thoughts will also be.　　MATTHEW 6:19-21

You know how full of love and kindness our Lord Jesus Christ was. Though he was very rich, yet for your sakes he became poor, so that by his poverty he could make you rich.　　2 CORINTHIANS 8:9

This same God who takes care of me will supply all your needs from his glorious riches, which have been given to us in Christ Jesus.　　PHILIPPIANS 4:19

Thirst-quenching
thought for the day

Jesus turned the values of the world upside down. He reminded people that the accepted foundation of human life—earthly treasures, or possessions—has no eternal shelf life. He pointed out that a foundation with rising and falling value easily becomes the entire focus of our "heart and thoughts." He also offered an infinitely better alternative: eternal treasure.

The world's idea of "rich" still includes money, possessions, and power. No wonder the world finds it difficult to understand and accept Christ. To Jesus, true riches include forgiveness, peace, purpose, and eternal life.

The Lord Jesus Christ set aside riches—his power and the glory of heaven—to become poor—living as a human being, suffering scorn and abuse, and dying on the cross. Now, because of what Jesus has done, we can share in God's wealth. That's the only treasure lasting enough to deserve our full attention.

Sip to take away
Regardless of the size of your bank account, house, and pile of earthly goods, you are rich in God's grace. Stack God's riches next to the world's—the difference is infinite.

a cup of . . .
Sacrificial Love

LIVING WATER

He was wounded and crushed for our sins. He was beaten that we might have peace. He was whipped, and we were healed! All of us have strayed away like sheep. We have left God's paths to follow our own. Yet the LORD laid on him the guilt and sins of us all.   ISAIAH 53:5-6

He was handed over to die because of our sins, and he was raised from the dead to make us right with God.   ROMANS 4:25

I passed on to you what was most important and what had also been passed on to me—that Christ died for our sins, just as the Scriptures said.

1 CORINTHIANS 15:3

Thirst-quenching thought for the day

Hundreds of years before Jesus' birth, Isaiah prophesied that our Lord would be pierced, crushed, punished, and wounded. Looking back centuries later, Paul knew that Jesus completely fulfilled all of these inspired predictions. We can hardly avoid the same conclusion.

On the cross, Jesus took the punishment that should have been ours for our transgressions and iniquities, bearing the scorn and pain and separation from his Father. Now, because of what Christ did, we can be forgiven, know peace with God, and have eternal life.

Sip to take away

When you feel weighed down by sin, stung by rebukes, burdened by cares, or torn by conflicts, remember Jesus and his sacrifice for you. He gave everything to bring you life. He loves you that much!

a cup of ...

Safety

LIVING WATER

O God, listen to my cry!
    Hear my prayer!
From the ends of the earth,
    I will cry to you for help,
    for my heart is overwhelmed.
Lead me to the towering rock of safety,
    for you are my safe refuge,
    a fortress where my enemies cannot reach me.
Let me live forever in your sanctuary,
    safe beneath the shelter of your wings!

PSALM 61:1-4

This I declare of the LORD:
    He alone is my refuge, my place of safety;
    he is my God, and I am trusting him.   PSALM 91:2

Thirst-quenching thought for the day

Remember watching your mother and father stand at the window and wave good-bye as you drove away from home? They became smaller and smaller until they disappeared from view as you sped off.

At times that's how it seems to be with God—fading into the background, distant, beyond our understanding and experience. Burdened by worries, overwhelmed by circumstances, besieged by temptation, or torn by guilt, we may forget his love and care as we speed on our way and put distance in the relationship.

Regardless of your location and situation, however, know that God is near. Even as David called "from the ends of the earth" emotionally, we can call on God in all situations. No matter where you are—physically, emotionally, or morally—you can never be lost to God's love. Your decision to call on him, no matter what the circumstances, will consistently deepen your sense of security in him. He will listen to your prayer.

Sip to take away

Remember that real safety has less to do with how you feel than with the One who provides your safety.

a cup of . . .

Salvation

LIVING WATER

We are made right in God's sight when we trust in Jesus Christ to take away our sins. And we all can be saved in this same way, no matter who we are or what we have done.   ROMANS 3:22

God is so rich in mercy, and he loved us so very much, that even while we were dead because of our sins, he gave us life when he raised Christ from the dead. (It is only by God's special favor that you have been saved!)   EPHESIANS 2:4-5

Then God our Savior showed us his kindness and love. He saved us, not because of the good things we did, but because of his mercy. He washed away our sins and gave us a new life through the Holy Spirit. He generously poured out the Spirit upon us because of what Jesus Christ our Savior did. He declared us not guilty because of his great kindness. And now we know that we will inherit eternal life.   TITUS 3:4-7

Thirst-quenching
thought for the day

"Brother, have you been saved?" shouts the curb-side preacher, and we cringe at his audacity and his confrontational approach.

Yet that is the important question, isn't it? If we have been saved (cleansed of all our sin through the blood of Christ), then we will be saved (live eternally in heaven with our Lord).

The great miracle of this salvation is that we can do absolutely nothing to earn it. We gain forgive-ness and eternal life through the generous kind-ness of God. His mercy and grace reach us wherever we are, whatever we have done.

Now justified, we stand clean in his presence.

Sip to take away

When you ache or stumble or doubt, remember that you are saved if you have turned your life over to Jesus!

a cup of . . .
Satisfaction

LIVING WATER

The poor will eat and be satisfied.
   All who seek the LORD will praise him.
   Their hearts will rejoice with everlasting joy.

PSALM 22:26

O God, you are my God;
   I earnestly search for you.
My soul thirsts for you;
   my whole body longs for you
in this parched and weary land
   where there is no water.

PSALM 63:1

Is anyone thirsty? Come and drink—even if you have
no money! Come, take your choice of wine or
milk—it's all free! Why spend your money on food
that does not give you strength? Why pay for food
that does you no good? Listen, and I will tell you
where to get food that is good for the soul!

ISAIAH 55:1-2

Thirst-quenching thought for the day

Imagine an oasis with tall palms, clear springs, and abundant food and drink. Offering satisfaction and even life, this sought-after spot in the sands would draw hungry and thirsty desert wanderers. Desperate and needy, they would expend every ounce of strength to get there.

Just as dry throats and parched lips yearn for drink, and empty stomachs and starved bodies cry for food, spiritually starved men and women seek sustenance. And like a glorious oasis, passages like these give hope. Here God offers satisfaction, renewal, and the real soul food—life. Other offers entice, but they prove to be only mirages. This oasis is real.

Sip to take away
Do you thirst? Drink God's water of life. Are you hungry? Pull up to his banquet table and feast on his goodness.

a cup of . . .

Secure Foundation

LIVING WATER

The LORD is my rock, my fortress, and my savior;
  my God is my rock, in whom I find protection.
He is my shield, the strength of my salvation, and
    my stronghold,
  my high tower, my savior, the one who saves me
    from violence.   2 SAMUEL 22:2-3

Be for me a great rock of safety,
  a fortress where my enemies cannot reach me.
You are my rock and my fortress.
  For the honor of your name, lead me out of this
    peril.   PSALM 31:2-3

Be to me a protecting rock of safety,
  where I am always welcome.
Give the order to save me,
  for you are my rock and my fortress.   PSALM 71:3

Thirst-quenching thought for the day

Toddlers clutch blankets, stuffed toys, unused cloth diapers, and other security symbols, dragging them wherever they go. They're cute, but that's because they're still young. Older children, teenagers, and adults acting similarly would be seen as mentally slow or emotionally weak. Yet today, many adults tightly clutch other, more acceptable, "security blankets": a special relationship, good health, a prestigious career, talent, prized possessions, money. Far from providing a secure foundation, however, each one of these "blankets" can be lost, stolen, or swept away, and each will fail when needed most.

In contrast, listen to these words of David as he describes his source of security: "rock," "fortress," "deliverer," "shield," "stronghold," "refuge," "savior." David knew from personal experience that God alone could secure his present and his future.

Sip to take away

What are you holding onto? What are you depending on? Build your life on the rock—God almighty. He's the only secure foundation.

a cup of . . .

Shade

LIVING WATER

How precious is your unfailing love, O God!
All humanity finds shelter
in the shadow of your wings.
You feed them from the abundance of your
own house,
letting them drink from your rivers of delight.

PSALM 36:7-8

Those who live in the shelter of the Most High
will find rest in the shadow of the Almighty.
This I declare of the LORD:
He alone is my refuge, my place of safety;
he is my God, and I am trusting him.
For he will rescue you from every trap
and protect you from the fatal plague.
He will shield you with his wings.
He will shelter you with his feathers.
His faithful promises are your armor and
protection.

PSALM 91:1-4

Thirst-quenching thought for the day

For God's people, who lived in a desert country, being able to rest in shade was important. David used the image of shade to describe God's protection of his people. He also used the following metaphors:

- "Shelter in the shadow of your wings": Like a baby bird who finds safety in the nest, God protects his own.

- "Feed them from the abundance of your house": As welcomed guests, God invites us to a lavish banquet table overflowing with blessings.

- "Drink from the rivers of delight": God's endless river brings refreshing, thirst-quenching joy.

- "My place of safety": God's presence creates a continual sense of shelter over our lives.

Sip to take away
The picture is clear—God is our comfort, protection, shade, and refreshment in the desert times of our lives.

a cup of . . .

Shepherding

LIVING WATER

The LORD is my shepherd;
* I have everything I need.*
He lets me rest in green meadows;
* he leads me beside peaceful streams.*   PSALM 23:1-2

I am the good shepherd. The good shepherd lays
down his life for the sheep.   JOHN 10:11

Once you were wandering like lost sheep. But now
you have turned to your Shepherd, the Guardian of
your souls.   1 PETER 2:25

Thirst-quenching thought for the day

Restoring an antique requires paint remover, hard work, and patience. Restoring an older home requires masonry, carpentry, plumbing, and electrical skills and a considerable investment of time, money, and energy. But what does it take to restore a dusty old soul?

When trials and time join forces to ravage us, tearing at body and mind and crushing the spirit, we desperately need restoration—to be refreshed and renewed and brought back to mint condition. But only the Lord can do that work. As our original designer and creator, only he knows us and has the necessary tools. Only he can restore our souls and renew our strength.

God begins his miracle of restoration by leading us, like a caring shepherd, away from the bustle and traffic, stress and storms, to green pastures where we can rest and be refreshed. And he leads us to the still waters—calm, quiet, deep, inviting—where we can quench our thirst and receive his loving care.

Sip to take away

Restoration begins when we stop running and struggling like frightened sheep and submit to the Good Shepherd. God wants to restore our souls, and he has everything we need.

a cup of...
Shielding

LIVING WATER

O LORD, I have so many enemies;
  so many are against me.
So many are saying,
  "God will never rescue him!"

You, O LORD, are a shield around me,
  my glory, and the one who lifts my head high.

PSALM 3:1-3

Those who hate me without cause
  are more numerous than the hairs on my head.
These enemies who seek to destroy me
  are doing so without cause.
They attack me with lies,
  demanding that I give back what I didn't steal....

Don't let those who trust in you stumble because
    of me,
  O Sovereign LORD Almighty.
Don't let me cause them to be humiliated,
  O God of Israel.

PSALM 69:4, 6

Thirst-quenching thought for the day

David wrote Psalm 3 while fleeing from Absalom. With his own son turning against him, David seemed to be completely surrounded by enemies. Even those who stood on his side expressed pessimism concerning the eventual outcome, doubting that even God could save him. Certainly David could have become utterly discouraged and hopeless.

Yet he confidently wrote that God would protect him, destroy his enemies, and restore him to his rightful place on the throne. David had no idea how this would happen—he was devastated politically, physically, and emotionally—but he knew who was in charge of his life and destiny.

Many people seem to spend their lives running and hiding, upset about the past, anxious about the present, and worried about the future. Seeing enemies everywhere, even in themselves, they hang their heads in shame and despair. David could have given up; instead, he found courage and hope in God.

Sip to take away
God is your shield. Trust him. He will bestow glory and lift your head.

a cup of . . .

Significance

LIVING WATER

When I look at the night sky and see the work of
*   your fingers—*
*   the moon and the stars you have set in place—*
what are mortals that you should think of us,
*   mere humans that you should care for us?*
For you made us only a little lower than God,
*   and you crowned us with glory and honor.*

PSALM 8:3-5

The heavens tell of the glory of God.
*   The skies display his marvelous craftsmanship.*
Day after day they continue to speak;
*   night after night they make him known.*
They speak without a sound or a word;
*   their voice is silent in the skies;*
yet their message has gone out to all the earth,
*   and their words to all the world.*   PSALM 19:1-4

Thirst-quenching thought for the day

Do you feel small and insignificant when you look up at the night sky and the expanse of stars? When you look down at the countless lights of urban sprawl? When you look around at crowds of people?

David had that feeling, yet he understood that in God's eyes he was important, created just a "little lower than God."

Every person, including you, is significant as God's special creation, crowned with glory and honor. In fact, as Psalm 19 notes, all of creation is a message written for the world to read. God thinks you are significant enough to receive his message.

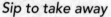

Sip to take away

Take another look at the moon and stars, and see the truth: The Creator of all that exists cares about you and is thinking about you. Then look at yourself as God does.

a cup of . . .

Sleep

LIVING WATER

I will lie down in peace and sleep,

for you alone, O LORD, will keep me safe. PSALM 4:8

I am leaving you with a gift—peace of mind and heart. And the peace I give isn't like the peace the world gives. So don't be troubled or afraid. JOHN 14:27

I have told you all this so that you may have peace in me. Here on earth you will have many trials and sorrows. But take heart, because I have overcome the world. JOHN 16:33

Thirst-quenching thought for the day

Fear moistens our palms, buckles our knees, and chokes our breath. Fear keeps us awake at night, robbing us of rest. Debilitating terror makes cowards of even the strongest and most powerful warriors. Some try to fight their fears by ignoring them. Others mask their fears through anesthesia (alcohol and drugs) or false bravado (pretending that all is well). Some respond by rushing recklessly into danger. But the answer, the effective antidote to fear, comes from knowing the truth, knowing what lies ahead, down the path.

Jesus told his disciples that he was the Truth (John 14:6) and that heaven awaited all who trusted in him (John 14:1-4). They did not need to fear, regardless of their circumstances, pressures, and troubles. Certainly these young men didn't know the future, but they knew the One who did—and he promised them peace.

Sip to take away

What fears steal your hope and keep you awake at night? Turn that fear over to the one who has overcome the world. Trust the Savior, and sleep like a baby.

a cup of...
Solace

LIVING WATER

God blesses those who mourn,
for they will be comforted. MATTHEW 5:4

All praise to the God and Father of our Lord Jesus
Christ. He is the source of every mercy and the God
who comforts us. He comforts us in all our troubles
so that we can comfort others. When others are
troubled, we will be able to give them the same
comfort God has given us. 2 CORINTHIANS 1:3-4

Thirst-quenching
thought for the day

Years ago, the chorus of a contemporary Christian song challenged Christians to "pass it on," to spread the message of God's profound love and incredible salvation to others. In effect, that is what Paul is urging in this last passage, explaining that one reason God comforts us is so that we can comfort others.

What comfort do we receive from God?

- When we feel lonely and isolated, God assures us of his presence.
- When we struggle against pressure and problems, God provides his power.
- When we despair of life on earth, God points to the hope of heaven.
- When we grieve over unbearable loss, God gives of himself.

In the same way, we can comfort others—by being with them, helping, giving words of encouragement, telling of eternal life, and pointing to the Savior.

Sip to take away
Who needs your comfort? Think of how God has comforted you and then pass on that comfort to others.

a cup of . . .
Solid Ground

LIVING WATER

I waited patiently for the LORD to help me,
  and he turned to me and heard my cry.
He lifted me out of the pit of despair,
  out of the mud and the mire.
He set my feet on solid ground
  and steadied me as I walked along.   PSALM 40:1-2

God is our refuge and strength,
  always ready to help in times of trouble.
So we will not fear, even if earthquakes come
  and the mountains crumble into the sea.
Let the oceans roar and foam.
  Let the mountains tremble as the waters surge!
                                        PSALM 46:1-3

Thirst-quenching thought for the day

Waiting takes patience, especially when we want help and answers immediately. And pain, problems, and pressures increase the difficulty, causing us to feel like there is nothing we can count on to help us.

We don't know the nature of the struggle that David faced before he finally heard from God. "Slimy pit," "mud," and "mire" seem to indicate, however, that it was extremely unpleasant. Yet David "waited patiently for the Lord." In the second psalm, David recognized that times of trouble, earthquakes, and trembling mountains are no reason to fear, since we trust in the Lord, "our refuge and strength." And David's patient reliance on God was rewarded.

Often God wants to teach us during those difficult times of waiting for answers, solutions, and resolutions. He wants us to learn that he is in control and that he alone is our sure foundation and ally.

Sip to take away

Are you waiting for God to act? for his answers? for his rescue? Keep crying for help, but as you cry, be patient. He will lift you up, set you on solid ground, and give you a place to stand.

a cup of . . .
Stillness

LIVING WATER

Be silent, and know that I am God!
  I will be honored by every nation.
  I will be honored throughout the world.

PSALM 46:10

Acknowledge that the LORD is God! He made us, and we are his. We are his people, the sheep of his pasture.

PSALM 100:3

The day is coming when your pride will be brought low and the LORD alone will be exalted. . . . The arrogance of all people will be brought low. Their pride will lie in the dust. The LORD alone will be exalted!

ISAIAH 2:11, 17

Thirst-quenching
thought for the day

"Stop!" "Be silent!" "Let go of your concerns!" These are alternate translations for the word traditionally rendered "Be still" in Psalm 46:10. Through this psalm writer, God tells us to take a significant break from the frantic pace and hectic schedule, to move away from society's deafening cacophony, to stop talking and start listening to him. Then, and only then, will we be positioned to get to know him, our eternal, all-powerful, all-knowing, ever-present God.

It's not easy to disengage, to slow down, or to be still. Thirsting for success and hungering for meaning, we push and strain and fill every waking moment with activity. We work hard to succeed in our own strength, in our own power, under our own control. But God will be exalted among the nations, and he will be exalted in the earth. Right now, he wants to be exalted in our lives.

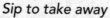 *Sip to take away*

Be still and silent—listen to God's gentle whisper.

Be still and silent—know that he alone is God.

Be still and silent—submit to him.

a cup of . . .

Strength

LIVING WATER

I love you, LORD; you are my strength.
The LORD is my rock, my fortress, and my savior;
    my God is my rock, in whom I find protection.
    He is my shield, the strength of my salvation, and
        my stronghold.
I will call on the LORD, who is worthy of praise,
    for he saves me from my enemies.   PSALM 18:1-3

You are my strength; I wait for you to rescue me,
    for you, O God, are my place of safety. . . .

O my Strength, to you I sing praises,
    for you, O God, are my refuge,
    the God who shows me unfailing love.

                                    PSALM 59:9, 17

Thirst-quenching thought for the day

King Saul had sent his men to capture and kill David. In the face of such deadly opposition and overwhelming odds, David could claim God as his place of safety, his "rock," and sing his praises.

Note that David wrote this psalm before being rescued. David's faith was unshakable. He trusted God to help him, but he knew that whatever happened, God, his strength, controlled his fate. That was a truth he could live with.

God doesn't promise to deliver us from every threat, but he does promise his love and presence. God doesn't promise us victory in every battle, but he does promise to work everything for our good. God doesn't promise earthly peace and prosperity, but he does promise life eternal.

Sip to take away
Regardless of the enemies who surround you, make God your strength and give him praise.

a cup of . . .
Support

LIVING WATER

Remember that the temptations that come into your life are no different from what others experience. And God is faithful. He will keep the temptation from becoming so strong that you can't stand up against it. When you are tempted, he will show you a way out so that you will not give in to it.

1 CORINTHIANS 10:13

Since he himself has gone through suffering and temptation, he is able to help us when we are being tempted.

HEBREWS 2:18

This High Priest of ours understands our weaknesses, for he faced all of the same temptations we do, yet he did not sin.

HEBREWS 4:15

Thirst-quenching
thought for the day

When Jesus became a human being, he had all the normal human needs and desires. As a baby, he had to be fed, dressed, held, and taught. Over the years he grew and matured as a boy and a young man. As a normal adolescent, Jesus experienced temptation. The Bible doesn't tell about his teenage years, but surely Jesus was tempted to disobey Mary and Joseph, to assert his independence, to lust, and to be filled with pride. Later, after his public baptism by John the Baptist, Jesus was led into the wilderness to be tempted one-on-one, face-to-face with Satan.

In all of these temptations, Jesus struggled and suffered, yet he resisted. He did not give in. He did not sin.

What temptations entice you? Jesus knows your struggle. First-century Jewish culture differed greatly from ours, but the basic temptations were the same: lying, stealing, hatred, pride, self-indulgence, worshiping other gods, materialism, and many more. Jesus can help you resist temptation's strong pull.

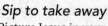

Sip to take away
Picture Jesus in your situation. How would he respond when tempted with what you are facing? Ask him to help you resist and follow his example.

a cup of . . .

Testing

LIVING WATER

Fire tests the purity of silver and gold, but the LORD tests the heart.   PROVERBS 17:3

When your faith is tested, your endurance has a chance to grow.   JAMES 1:3

These trials are only to test your faith, to show that it is strong and pure. It is being tested as fire tests and purifies gold—and your faith is far more precious to God than mere gold. So if your faith remains strong after being tried by fiery trials, it will bring you much praise and glory and honor on the day when Jesus Christ is revealed to the whole world.   1 PETER 1:7

Thirst-quenching thought for the day

Those "tests" and "trials" mentioned by James and Peter refer to the many difficulties that Christians were experiencing. Many faced discrimination, verbal and physical abuse, and even torture and death. Peter's inspired message to these beleaguered believers reminded them that God was using their trials to refine their faith. Thus, they should stand strong, keeping their eyes on Christ.

Modern persecutions often come in more subtle forms: social pressure, sarcasm, interpersonal conflicts, and even legal restraints. But these also cause pain, and we can become weary of defending ourselves and our Lord.

Who hassles you? What pressures and problems do you face? How are you suffering? Whatever the persecution, know that God is using it to build your faith and to conform you to the image of his Son (see Romans 8:29).

Sip to take away

Let those around you know that your faith is genuine and "of greater worth than gold." Take hope, knowing that all will be made right when your Savior is revealed.

a cup of…
Thanksgiving

LIVING WATER

The LORD is my strength, my shield from every
*   danger.*
*   I trust in him with all my heart.*
He helps me, and my heart is filled with joy.
*   I burst out in songs of thanksgiving.* PSALM 28:7

Always be full of joy in the Lord. I say it
again—rejoice! Let everyone see that you are consid-
erate in all you do. Remember, the Lord is coming
soon. Don't worry about anything; instead, pray
about everything. Tell God what you need, and
thank him for all he has done. PHILIPPIANS 4:4-6

Always be joyful. Keep on praying. No matter what
happens, always be thankful, for this is God's will
for you who belong to Christ Jesus.

1 THESSALONIANS 5:16-18

Thirst-quenching thought for the day

These verses contain three commands that seem impossible to obey. The difficulty lies in the expressions "always," "keep on," and "no matter what happens." We wonder how we can perpetually rejoice, pray, and be thankful, especially when encountering painful trials, perplexing problems, and extreme conflicts. Yet this is what God wants us to do—it is his will.

The last phrase of this verse—"who belong to Christ Jesus"—holds the answer. When we consider Christ's work on the cross in the past, his intercession for us right now, and what he has promised to do for us in the future, we can "be joyful" and "give thanks" continually because we are his.

Joy flows from knowing that God loves us. Thanks comes from knowing that God is working in our lives in each and every circumstance. Praying continually is a natural response for those in close relationship with their Creator and Savior.

Sip to take away

Focus on Christ and live with joy, knowing that whatever happens to us, God is with us and working out his best for us (see Romans 8:28).

a cup of . . .

Transparency

LIVING WATER

But the LORD said to Samuel, "Don't judge by his appearance or height, for I have rejected him. The LORD doesn't make decisions the way you do! People judge by outward appearance, but the LORD looks at a person's thoughts and intentions."   1 SAMUEL 16:7

Hear from heaven where you live, and forgive. Give your people whatever they deserve, for you alone know the human heart. Then they will fear you and walk in your ways as long as they live in the land you gave to our ancestors.   1 KINGS 8:39-40

Jesus didn't trust them, because he knew what people were really like. No one needed to tell him about human nature.   JOHN 2:24-25

Thirst-quenching thought for the day

The Scriptures repeatedly demonstrate that God knows people inside out. God sent Samuel to Bethlehem to anoint one of Jesse's sons as the next king of Israel. Samuel naturally assumed that the next king would be tall, handsome, and strong, like Israel's first king, Saul. Isn't that how kings are supposed to be?

"But the LORD looks at a person's thoughts and intentions." The next king would not be Eliab, or Abinadab, or any of the seven older brothers. Instead, God chose the youngest—David the shepherd boy.

Society still values outward appearances. Plaudits and power still come to the "beautiful people"—athletes and media celebrities with exceptional physical characteristics. With such men and women presented as ideals, it's easy to feel ugly, unwanted, insignificant, and worthless in comparison.

But God's standards have not changed. Regardless of outward appearance, he looks at the inside of a person, examining desires, motives, character, attitudes, and faith.

 Sip to take away

Expend your energy on developing inner beauty. That's what matters to God, and his opinion is what truly matters. Remember, he knows your heart.

a cup of . . .

Trust

LIVING WATER

When I am afraid,
  I put my trust in you.
O God, I praise your word.
  I trust in God, so why should I be afraid?
  What can mere mortals do to me?   PSALM 56:3-4

The LORD is for me, so I will not be afraid.
  What can mere mortals do to me?
Yes, the LORD is for me; he will help me.
  I will look in triumph at those who hate me.
It is better to trust the LORD
  than to put confidence in people.
It is better to trust the LORD
  than to put confidence in princes.   PSALM 118:6-9

Thirst-quenching thought for the day

The familiar phrase stamped on all U.S. coins reads, "In God we trust." For most, that's merely a motto, a nice sentiment with very little basis in reality. But David lived this motto. Fleeing from Saul, he had taken refuge in Philistine territory. Thus, he had escaped from one enemy only to fall into the hands of another. From a purely human perspective, he was doomed. There was no way out.

Certainly David must have been afraid. Yet in his fear he could affirm his strong trust in God. David knew God and he knew that he could trust God's word. The more David thought about his loving heavenly Father, the less he worried about his circumstances and his enemies. After all, what could "mortal man" do to him?

Sip to take away

How are you trusting these days? Are you nervous, anxious, concerned, fearful? Take a realistic look at your situation, but then look at God, who has the power and the will to act on your behalf.

a cup of . . .

Unburdening

LIVING WATER

Give your burdens to the LORD,
and he will take care of you.
He will not permit the godly to slip and fall.

PSALM 55:22

The LORD opens the eyes of the blind.
The LORD lifts the burdens of those bent beneath
their loads.
The LORD loves the righteous.   PSALM 146:8

Jesus said, "Come to me, all of you who are weary
and carry heavy burdens, and I will give you rest."

MATTHEW 11:28

Thirst-quenching thought for the day

Have you carried a heavy bag or backpack on your shoulder for a long distance recently? After a while you seem to bend a bit lower with every labored step. Finally, upon reaching your destination, you summon the strength, and with a push and a grunt you drop the load where it belongs. What a relief! What a feeling of freedom!

Much like that great load, cares and anxieties often weigh us down, slowing our pace and stooping our shoulders. We worry about the future, finances, family, and friendships. We question past actions and fear coming events. No wonder ulcers, migraines, and insomnia are epidemic.

God urges us to give our burdens to him instead of struggling under that overwhelming weight. God wants to free us to walk fearlessly and confidently, upright and strong, while he bears the load. He's strong enough to lift and carry anything we give him.

Sip to take away

What heavy weight do you carry? What causes your sleepless nights and restless days? What pushes you to the brink? Let God carry your burdens—he will sustain you and keep you standing tall.

a cup of...

Undeserved Favor

LIVING WATER

You have every spiritual gift you need as you eagerly wait for the return of our Lord Jesus Christ. He will keep you strong right up to the end, and he will keep you free from all blame on the great day when our Lord Jesus Christ returns. God will surely do this for you, for he always does just what he says, and he is the one who invited you into this wonderful friendship with his Son, Jesus Christ our Lord.

1 CORINTHIANS 1:7-9

May the God of peace make you holy in every way, and may your whole spirit and soul and body be kept blameless until that day when our Lord Jesus Christ comes again. God, who calls you, is faithful; he will do this.

1 THESSALONIANS 5:23-24

Thirst-quenching
thought for the day

The Corinthian church was struggling with conflict
and division. Yet in the verses preceding these
(1 Corinthians 1:4-6), Paul affirmed God's work for
and in the believers there. They had been "enriched"
in their "eloquence" and "knowledge," and they had
every necessary "spiritual gift." In addition, Paul
reminded them that God would keep them "strong
right up to the end" and "free from all blame."

From these passages it becomes obvious that the
Christian life depends totally on God. He calls, gives
faith, saves by faith, confirms salvation, distributes
spiritual gifts, strengthens, and keeps till the end.

God's favor is undeserved. Earning it is impossible—in the first century and today, for the Corinthians and for you. That's grace. And God is faithful.
No one holds on to God; he does the holding
and keeping.

Sip to take away

Regardless of your past sins or present
condition, if you have trusted in Christ as
Savior, God is working in you to conform
you to Christ's image (see Romans
8:29). So stop struggling and start
living for him.

a cup of...
Unexpected Relief

LIVING WATER

And Miriam sang this song:

"I will sing to the LORD, for he has triumphed gloriously;
he has thrown both horse and rider into the sea."

EXODUS 15:21

You displayed miraculous signs and wonders against Pharaoh, his servants, and all his people, for you knew how arrogantly the Egyptians were treating them. You have a glorious reputation that has never been forgotten. You divided the sea for your people so they could walk through on dry land! And then you hurled their enemies into the depths of the sea.

NEHEMIAH 9:10-11

Thirst-quenching thought for the day

After having endured decades of slavery and then having watched ten plagues devastate the country while Pharaoh's heart hardened before their eyes, the children of Israel had finally been allowed to leave Egypt and travel to their Promised Land. Yet looking back from the edge of the Red Sea, they saw the dust from Egyptian horses' hooves. Pharaoh had again changed his mind and was pursuing them with deadly intent. Despair seemed about to overwhelm hope.

Then God parted the waters, and his people walked to freedom on dry ground. When he released the waters, the pursuing army drowned.

What relief! What joy! What gratitude! Moses and Miriam led the people in praise to God, who had delivered them. Nehemiah remembered this event and recounted how surprised they were by God's unexpected rescue. We can always expect God to answer, but the way God answers often will catch us by surprise!

Sip to take away

Who stands as your Pharaoh, enslaving you and defying God? Remember that your Lord fights your battles and will bring you to the place you are to go. Praise him for his strength and guidance and step out in faith. Count on his unexpected relief.

a cup of...

Value

LIVING WATER

God created people in his own image;
God patterned them after himself;
male and female he created them. GENESIS 1:27

You made all the delicate, inner parts of my body
and knit me together in my mother's womb.
Thank you for making me so wonderfully complex!
Your workmanship is marvelous—and how well I
know it.
You watched me as I was being formed in utter
seclusion,
as I was woven together in the dark of the womb.
You saw me before I was born.
Every day of my life was recorded in your book.
Every moment was laid out
before a single day had passed. PSALM 139:13-16

Thirst-quenching thought for the day

"You're nothing! You're hopeless! You're useless!"

Whether shouted, spoken, or implied, cutting statements like these wound deeply.

But these verses, nestled among others in God's Word, shout just the opposite about people. You have value! You count! As a descendent of the first parents, you are God's special creation, made in his image. Thus, in some way, you are like God. You are unique in creation as one who can have a personal relationship with the Creator. You are unique among humans because God specifically designed you.

If you think these verses are too good to be true, read the rest of the Bible. You will discover covenant promises, redemption, grace, mercy, forgiveness, salvation, and guidance—everything you need to live as a unique creation of God.

Sip to take away

Regardless of painful circumstances and hateful words, know that you have worth. God created you, and he loves you. Let that truth sink into your soul, and then bask in his love and live as his special child.

a cup of . . .
Victory

LIVING WATER

[The priest] will say, "Listen to me, all you men of Israel! Do not be afraid as you go out to fight today! Do not lose heart or panic. For the LORD your God is going with you! He will fight for you against your enemies, and he will give you victory!"

DEUTERONOMY 20:3-4

I command you—be strong and courageous! Do not be afraid or discouraged. For the LORD your God is with you wherever you go. JOSHUA 1:9

Thirst-quenching thought for the day

God told the priest to explain to the Israelite soldiers that the one who had brought them out of Egypt was always with them. Regardless of the enemy, they need not fear because God would fight with them and for them, assuring them of victory. God gave Joshua the same assurance.

Enemies continue to threaten God's people: financial struggles, failing health, job stress, family conflict, persecution. Normal reactions to such daunting battles include frustration, fear, and often, outright terror. The way to deal with these problems is not to deny the power or reality of what threatens us, but rather to rely on the resources we have in God. God tells us to recall his previous work—past assurances of his presence and demonstrations of his power—and to know that this same powerful and loving God is with us today, in this battle.

Sip to take away

What enemy do you face today? Don't panic. God still has all the power, and he will fight for you, because he loves you. Move forward in faith toward victory.

a cup of...

Vindication

LIVING WATER

The LORD reigns forever,
  executing judgment from his throne.
He will judge the world with justice
  and rule the nations with fairness.
The LORD is a shelter for the oppressed,
  a refuge in times of trouble.
Those who know your name trust in you,
  for you, O LORD, have never abandoned anyone
    who searches for you.   PSALM 9:7-10

In his justice he will punish those who persecute
you. And God will provide rest for you who are being
persecuted and also for us when the Lord Jesus
appears from heaven. He will come with his
mighty angels,   2 THESSALONIANS 1:6-7

Thirst-quenching thought for the day

These last words were written to first-century followers of Christ who were living as a small minority in a world violently opposed to their faith. Persecuted and harassed, many believers were rejected by family and friends and denied employment. Others suffered great physical harm. They looked for rescue, and they yearned for justice.

They heard good news from Paul—God is just. He knew about their suffering, and eventually those believers would be rewarded for their faithfulness.

Pressed on every side, do you cry out for relief from trials, troubles, and persecution? At times, a seemingly endless horde of problems and pressures surround like a hostile army, threatening to attack and destroy. You can see no exit, no hope, only disaster and defeat. Listen to Paul's clear word—God is just. Eventually accounts will be settled, wrongs will be righted, and the righteous will be vindicated.

Sip to take away

Acknowledge God's justice in your own life. Choose an area in which you know you've been wronged, and place that matter in God's hands. Prayerfully leave the resolution with him.

a cup of . . .

Welcome

LIVING WATER

*The Lord's voice will roar from Zion and thunder
from Jerusalem, and the earth and heavens will
begin to shake. But to his people of Israel, the LORD
will be a welcoming refuge and a strong fortress.*

JOEL 3:16

*He returned home to his father. And while he was
still a long distance away, his father saw him
coming. Filled with love and compassion, he ran to
his son, embraced him, and kissed him.*   LUKE 15:20

*Because of Christ and our faith in him, we can now
come fearlessly into God's presence, assured of his
glad welcome.*   EPHESIANS 3:12

Thirst-quenching
thought for the day

In the happy ending to Jesus' marvelous parable of the lost son (Luke 15:11-32), the father sees the son from "a long distance away." Thus, he must have been looking daily for his wayward boy. When the son appeared, the father dropped everything and ran to him.

Where are you in the story? Perhaps, like the lost son, you are ready to leave home. Tired of the restrictions and rules, you want to go your own way. Maybe you are in the "far country" (Luke 15:13), far from home and having a ball. Perhaps you are in the pigpen—broke, hungry, and painfully aware of what you left behind. Maybe you're headed back, rehearsing your speech of repentance.

Wherever you are, your loving Father waits for your return. Standing at the edge of the yard, peering into the distance, he looks for your familiar form. Filled with compassion, he is ready to welcome you back.

Sip to take away
Today, remember that the best thing the son did was turn around. The father couldn't meet him until he turned and returned.

a cup of . . .

Worship

LIVING WATER

Stand up and praise the LORD your God, for he lives from everlasting to everlasting! . . . Praise his glorious name! It is far greater than we can think or say. You alone are the LORD. You made the skies and the heavens and all the stars. You made the earth and the seas and everything in them. You preserve and give life to everything, and all the angels of heaven worship you.   NEHEMIAH 9:5-6

Praise the LORD, you angels of his,
    you mighty creatures who carry out his plans,
    listening for each of his commands.
Yes, praise the LORD, you armies of angels
    who serve him and do his will!
Praise the LORD, everything he has created,
    everywhere in his kingdom.
    As for me—I, too, will praise the LORD.

PSALM 103:19-22

Thirst-quenching thought for the day

Nehemiah had returned to Jerusalem. With courage, tenacity, and strong leadership, he organized the people to rebuild the city walls. Afterward, they worshiped God together.

It must have been a remarkable scene. When Ezra read from the book of the law, many wept, realizing that they were sinful people. (It was the first time that some had ever understood God's Word.) Then, after confessing their sins, they praised their eternal and glorious Lord for his love, forgiveness, and work in their lives.

Genuine worship and praise overflows from a grateful heart. Psalm 103 makes the same point. When people truly understand the gravity of their sin and the depth of God's love, they cannot help but stand and shout praises to the Lord. Then they make the life changes that God requires.

Sip to take away

If your fervor has cooled or you feel far from God, reread the passages in his Word that remind you of his nature and his work. Then join the "multitudes of heaven"—stand up and praise the Lord your God, who is from everlasting to everlasting.

Subject Index

Scripture Index